Ightfield Church

THE OLD PARISH CHURCHES

OF SHROPSHIRE

Mike Salter

FOLLY PUBLICATIONS

ACKNOWLEDGEMENTS

All photographs, brass rubbings and old postcards in this book are reproduced from originals in the author's collection. He also drew the plans and map. Thanks to Mary Doncaster for help with accommodation and transport during work on this edition. This book is dedicated to my uncle, the late Roy Guest, who farmed at Nine Springs, Clee Hill during the 1950s, and then moved to Howle, near Newport. The costs of printing were covered by a legacy under the will of another relative, Pat Baily.

AUTHOR'S NOTES

This series of books (see full list inside the back cover) are intended as portable field guides giving as much information and illustrative material as possible in volumes of modest size, weight and price. As a whole the series gives a lot of information on lesser known buildings rather than concentrating on the well known ones which have mostly been adequately described elsewhere. As with the other church books in the series this volume concentrates on the period before the Industrial Revolution of the late 18th century necessitated the construction of many new 19th century churches to serve expanding urban areas. Most furnishings and monuments after 1800 are not mentioned, although additions and alterations to older churches usually are. Churches founded after 1800 are not mentioned in the gazetteers, nor do they appear on the map, but they are listed with brief details at the back of the book.

This book is inevitably very much a catalogue of descriptions, dates and names. It is intended as a field guide and for reference rather than to be read from start to finish. Occasionally there are comments about the settings of churches but on the whole lack of space permits little to be said about their position or atmosphere. Occasionally the most interesting features of a church or graveyard may lie outside the scope of this book as outlined above. The gazetteer features Ordnance Survey grid references (these are the two letters and six digits which appear after each place-name and dedication) and is intended to be used in conjunction with O.S. 1:50,000 scale maps. These are vital for finding churches in urban and remote locations.

Plans redrawn from originals drawn by the author in the 1970s are reproduced at a common scale of 1:400. The buildings were measured in metres and only metric scales are given. For those who need to convert three metres is almost ten feet. A system of hatching common to all the church plans in the books in this series is used to denote different periods of work. Where this is the case refer to another page. The plans should be treated with some caution. Some features are difficult to date and others are not easy to depict on small scale drawings, such as stones of one period being re-used in a later period, sometimes in a different place.

ABOUT THE AUTHOR

Mike Salter id 47 and has been a professional author-publisher since he went on the Government Enterprise Allowance Scheme for unemployed people in 1988. He is particularly interested in the planning and layout of medieval buildings and has a huge collection of plans of churches and castles he has measured during tours (mostly by bicycle and motorcycle) of all parts of the British Isles since 1968. Wolverhampton born and bred, Mike now lives in an old cottage beside the Malvern Hills. His other interests include walking, maps, railways, board games, morris dancing, playing percussion instruments and calling folk dances with a ceilidh band.

Copyright M.Salter 2001. First edition published 1988. This edition published 2001. Folly Publications, Folly Cottage, 151 West Malvern Rd, Malvern, Worcs WR14 4AY Printed by Aspect Design, 89 Newtown Rd, Malvern, Worcs WR14 2PD

Interior of Holy Cross Abbey Church, Shrewsbury

CONTENTS

Inside the front cover is a map of churches in the gazetteer.

INTRODUCTION

In Saxon times what later became the county of Shropshire formed the western edge of the kingdom of Mercia, where the Christian faith was firmly established by the late 7th century. Nothing as early as this remains in any of the churches, and it is likely that many of the early churches were timber framed and all remains of them have long vanished as a result of later rebuilding and extensions. The chancel at Barrow and the nave north wall at Diddlebury may be 10th century. Each has a window with a wide splay inwards and outwards from an opening midway in the wall thickness. At Stanton Lacy the nave and north transept remain from an early 11th century cruciform church with a central tower as wide as the nave and a narrower chancel. There is also Saxon walling in the naves at Rushbury and Wroxeter, whilst Diddlebury and Wroxeter have reset fragments of finely decorated preaching crosses. Excavation has revealed evidence of a tiny Saxon chancel at Claverley and of a nave and eastern apse at St Mary's at Shrewsbury. The church at Clun and the other Shrewsbury churches of St Alkmund, St Chad and St Julian are known to be of Saxon origin but have no remains of that period.

After their conquest of England in 1066 the Normans formed mostly a ruling minority, and few of them were craftsmen. Saxon masons remained at work alongside Normans so that there is an overlap period from c1050 up to 1100 in which features of both the Saxon and Norman styles can be seen. Of c1050-80 are the nave at Barrow and the nave west wall at Stottesdon with a doorway surmounted by a very crude tympanum, and both churches have Early Norman west towers of c1100 with later top stages. Uppington has an Early Norman tympanum, and at Clee St Margaret, Culmington, Pitchford, Sidbury and Stanton-upon-Hine-Heath there is probably late 11th century herringbone masonry with courses of stones angled in alternate directions at 45 degrees, whilst pre-Conquest masonry of this type remains at Diddlebury and Rushbury. Diddlebury has a 12th century tower built over the remains of a Late Saxon or Early Norman west porch or tower.

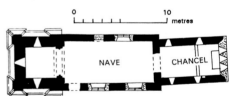

Plan of Linley Church

Hope Bagot Church

Heath Chapel

Interior of Much Wenlock Church

Half of the churches described in the gazetteer have structural remains from the 12th century, when there was a boom in new church construction, and the parochial system as we know it today, which began to take shape in the Late Saxon period, was completed. Very few new churches were established between the period of Magna Carta (1215) and the new series of churches built in the 19th century to serve new towns which sprang up as a result of the Industrial Revolution. The high proportion of 12th century work remaining in Shropshire churches is because the county has remained mostly pastoral with little population growth in many of the villages, especially those in hilly areas of marginal land. Many English churches were enlarged by adding aisles in the later medieval period but in Shropshire later generations were content to add just larger new windows, new roofs, towers, porches, the occasional chantry chapel, furnishings and memorials, and to replace as necessary crumbling exterior sandstone or limestone walling. Of Shropshire's parochial churches predating the late 18th century only a tenth have both north and south aisles to the nave, whilst another tenth has a an aisle on one side only. Amongst the small churches set fairly closely together in the hills west and south of the River Severn aisles are almost unknown.

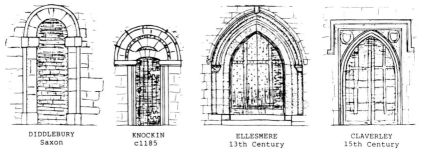

DIDDLEBURY
Saxon

KNOCKIN
c1185

ELLESMERE
13th Century

CLAVERLEY
15th Century

Church Doorways

Longford Church

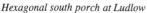
Hexagonal south porch at Ludlow

The most important work of the period 1100-40 is the aisled nave with round arches on large circular piers of the church of Shrewsbury Abbey. Some work at Morville, Linley and Astley Abbots relates to known consecration dates of 1118 and 1138. The Bishop of Hereford encouraged the building of new churches during the unrest of the late 1130s, when civil war was raging between King Stephen and the Empress Matilda, and people were unwilling to travel far to worship. Most of the work described as Norman in the gazetteer dates from c1140-85. Only a few examples can be mentioned here. There were cruciform churches with central towers at Condover and Ludlow, and at St Mary's at Shrewsbury, where rather more has survived. Otherwise all the churches conformed to a basic plan of a rectangular nave with a nearly square chancel typified by the almost unaltered churches of Heath and Aston Eyre. The main doorway was almost always on the south side. This doorway and the arch connecting the nave and chancel often have columns on each side and several orders of arches decorated with chevrons (zig-zag), heads, crenellation, and other motifs, as in the south doorway at Holdgate and the chancel arch at Stirchley. The semi-circular top is sometimes filled with a tympanum which often bears a pattern, as at Linley, or a piece of relief sculpture, as at Linley again and Aston Eyre. By c1185 towers had been added to the churches of Alveley, Clun, Diddlebury, Ditton Priors, Linley, Morville, Munslow, Neen Savage, St Mary's at Shrewsbury, and probably Bishop's Castle. The spacious church at Much Wenlock has a magnificent west facade, masked by a slightly later west tower, and evidence of an intended tower in an unusual SW corner position instead of in the most common place at the west end. Chelmarsh has some masonry remaining of the north aisle and Claverley and West Felton have round-arched arcades on thick round piers of north aisles otherwise rebuilt in later centuries.

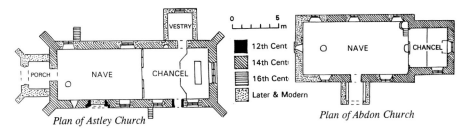

Plan of Astley Church

Plan of Abdon Church

During the period 1180-1200 there is a gradual change towards the Gothic style. Arches and jambs began to have chamfered edges and piers became more slender or of more complex section and have more delicate capitals decorated with leaf-like shapes, whilst round and pointed arches are used together as in the towers at Albrighton and Much Wenlock. Other west towers of this period are at Cleobury Mortimer, High Ercall, Lydbury North, Rushbury and Silvington. At Claverley and Eaton-under-Haywood the towers were placed on the south side because of the steep fall of the ground at the west end, whilst at Worthen, for no obvious reason, the tower was placed on the north side. An earlier church at Wrockwardine was given a central tower with transepts and a new chancel and at Wistanstow there is a complete cruciform church of c1190-1210 with pointed heads to most of the openings. There are remains of aisles of c1185-1200 at Alveley, Baschurch, Kinlet, Knockin, Morville, Shawbury, Stottesdon, West Felton, High Ercall and Clun, the last two having the more up-to-date pointed arches. The naves at Ashford Carbonell, Billingsley, Cardington and Clunbury were lengthened westwards c1180-1200 and four other Norman naves, plus the Saxon nave at Wroxeter, were also lengthened later on. Edstaston has an ornate and chancel built in two separate campaigns from c1175 onwards. This church, plus the tiny chapel at Cold Weston, the wide chancels added c1175-90 at Lydbury North, Diddlebury, Neen Savage and Wroxeter are all without chancel arches, the division between nave and chancel being marked only by later screens. Lastly there are the unusual two-storied church of c1190-1210 at Stapleton with pointed leaded lancet windows, and the wall painting of a battle scene of c1200 at Claverley, the only wall painting of note remaining in Shropshire.

Nearly a third of the churches described in the gazetteer have work of the 13th century. St Mary's at Shrewsbury has two aisles, and Alveley and Kinlet each have a south aisle with round-arched arcades of c1200-10, but after then openings normally have pointed arches. At Child's Ercall, Chirbury and Shifnal there are both north and south aisles of c1220-50, and there are single aisles at Aston Botterell, Cleobury Mortimer, Diddlebury, Ditton Priors, Much Wenlock and other places. There are fine, spacious south porches at Cleobury Mortimer, Kinlet, St Mary's at Shrewsbury and Shifnal. The Shifnal porch is rib-vaulted and has an original upper room which also extends over the adjacent bay of the south aisle. There is also an original north porch at the cruciform church of the 1270s at Acton Burnell, the finest and most complete 13th century church in Shropshire. Earlier churches made cruciform with central towers during this period are Church Stretton and Ellesmere. There are west towers at Atcham and Kinlet, the former with a fine west doorway, a huge but somewhat rebuilt SW corner tower at Oswestry, a tower of the 1290s in a transeptal position at Alberbury, and eighteen other minor or much-altered towers of this period. Church Preen, Leebotwood, Longnor, Lydham and Woolstaston have simple plain rectangular 13th century churches, and much of the churches at Bitterley and Pitchford are 13th century. The chancels at Alveley, Cardington, Culmington, Holdgate and Shawbury are of c1220-50, whilst the chancels at Atcham and Stanton Lacy and the unusually wide unaisled nave at Worthen are of later in the century.

Much Wenlock

Bitterley

Cleobury Mortimer

Ludlow

Whitchurch

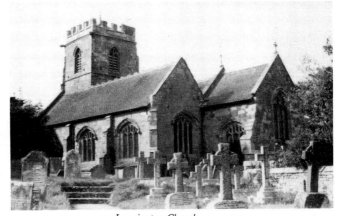

Window at Church Preen   *Loppington Church*

Towards the end of the 13th century the simple Early English style developed into the florid mature Gothic style known in England as Decorated. A quarter of Shropshire's parish churches have 14th century work in them, but much of it is only minor alterations to older work. The period starts with the small cruciform church at Neen Sollars, the central tower at Shifnal, the west tower at Chirbury, the north aisle and chapel at Cleobury Mortimer, and the nave and chancel at Clungunford, which are all of c1290-1310. A new north aisle, transepts, and a rare hexagonal porch were built at Ludlow c1310-40. The aisle west window has ballflower ornamentation, a characteristic of the Decorated style seen also on a number of tomb recesses, as at Culmington. Of that period also are the new chancels at Albrighton, Claverley, Edgmond, Kinlet and Stottesdon, and extensions of older chancels at Burford, Lilleshall, and Shifnal. In some of these the ogival arch, another characteristic of the Decorated period, begins to appear. Most of the wide-aisled church at Worfield is 14th century, and there are single aisles at Alberbury, Hodnet, Moreton Corbet, Ruyton and Stanton Lacy, a new arcade for an older aisle at Chelmarsh, transepts at Kinlet and Stanton Lacy, and small simple complete churches at Kinnersley, Nash and Abdon, the last two subsequently much altered. Shropshire has few 14th century towers but there are notable examples at Culmington, Market Drayton, Newport and Wem. Little work in the county can be safely assigned to the second half of the 14th century. Of the 1340s and 50s are the large south chapel at St Mary's Shrewsbury, most of the church at Hughley, and the rare octagonal west tower at Hodnet. The tower and many windows at Shrewsbury Abbey are of the 1360s, whilst the SW tower and spire at Worfield dates from c1370-90.

Tower at Worfield

Shropshire has two fine early 15th century collegiate churches. Battlefield was a completely new church erected by Henry IV to commemorate his victory over the Percies in 1403 and has a wide single chamber without aisles. The church lies alone and did not serve a village. At Tong an older church was rebuilt with an aisled nave, chancel and short transepts with a central tower which turns octagonal above the crossing. A third collegiate church serving the town at Newport was a larger building but has been mostly rebuilt in the 19th century. These churches were designed in the style now known as Perpendicular, which was introduced to Shropshire in the work of the 1360s at Shrewsbury Abbey, and which remained in vogue until the 1530s. The emphasised verticals and glasshouse effect of the style is shown off best at Ludlow, where in 1420-70 the transepts were raised, the chancel lengthened and a new lofty central tower, nave arcades and clerestory were built. Otherwise work of this period in Shropshire is mostly confined to the insertion of new windows and the addition of west towers. A few towers in the flatter, richer NE part of the county have a quatrefoil frieze below the battlements but non compare with the many fine towers of East Anglia or Somerset. Of the 15th century are the towers at Battlefield, Cheswardine, Edgmond, Highley, Ightfield, Kinnerley, Loppington, Upton Magna, Norton-in-Hales, Ruyton, Shawbury, Stockton and St Alkmund's at Shrewsbury, whilst those of Child's Ercall, Lilleshall, Moreton Corbet, St Martin's and Wroxeter may be as late as the 1520s or 30s. The only late medieval aisles are at Ightfield, Loppington and St Martins, and those at Edgmond which replaced 13th century aisles. More important is the small but internally spectacular chapel of 1515 at Tong with a fan-vaulted ceiling and there is a chapel of c1540-50 at Ludford.

At Melverley and Halston there are late medieval wooden framed chapels, and there are a number of timber-framed porches, belfries, and spires. Stone spires are rare in Shropshire, with just 14th century examples at Culmington and Worfield, the short example at Tong, and the splendid 15th century spires of St Mary's and St Alkmund's dominating the skyline of the town of Shrewsbury.

Interior of Whitchurch Church

English parish churches have many furnishings, monuments and roofs dating from the period 1550-1700 but little structural work apart from the occasional and mostly unimportant tower, porch, vestry or chapel. The only structural relics of Elizabeth I's reign in Shropshire are the small chapel-of-ease at Langley, the chancel at Shipton, the north transept at Shifnal, and the tower at Sutton Maddock. The churches of Loughton and Astley Abbots were rebuilt respectively in 1622 and 1633, and a tower was added at Myddle in 1634. Adderley, Lydbury North and More have early 17th century transeptal chapels which contained private pews for their respective lords of the manor. The recessed pyramidal timber tower tops at Clun and More are also probably early 17th century. Shropshire churches suffered unusually severely during the Civil Wars of the 1640s, after which Benthall, Bishop's Castle, High Ercall, Oswestry, Shrawardine and Stokesay all required substantial rebuilding. Condover gained a wide new nave and west tower in the 1660s after the collapse of the original central tower. Little Wenlock has a tower of 1667, Great Bolas has a late 17th century chancel, and in 1689 Minsterley was given a remarkable new church with Baroque motifs, a rarity in England, whilst Berwick has a private chapel of 1672.

More work survives from the 18th century than the previous two centuries. Whitchurch has a major aisled early 18th century church, and there are complete aisleless churches at Eyton-upon-the-Weald-Moors, Fitz, Hinstock, Hopton Cangford, Longdon-on-Tern, Montford, Preston-on-the-Weald-Moors, Ryton and Sibdon Carwood. Considerable parts of the churches Great Bolas, Kinnerley, Myddle, Quatford, Quatt, Selattyn and Stirchley are 18th century, and there are west towers at a dozen other churches, notably Adderley, Berwick, Sheriffhales and Whittington. From the 1790s there are major new classical style churches at Bridgnorth, Shrewsbury (the circular St Chad), and Wellington, and a minor church at Weston.

The earliest and the simplest form of church roof was the trussed rafter type, the framing of which usually looks seven sided from below. The roof at Wistanstow is possibly as early as c1200 and that at Church Stretton may be only slightly later. A common form from the 14th century onwards has collar beams and arched braces and tiers of wind braces cusped to form quatrefoil shapes. Good examples are at Alberbury, Clun and Hopesay. From about 1400 onwards appear very low pitched roofs with moulded beams and carved bosses, as at St Mary's Shrewsbury (nave), Ellesmere (south chapel) and Eaton-under-Haywood (chancel). Hammerbeam roofs, although a medieval idea, only came into fashion in Shropshire long after the Reformation of the 1530s. The wide nave of the 1660s at Condover has a good example.

Minsterley Church

Child's Ercall

```
0                    10
|_|_|_|_|_|_____|
        metres
```

Plan of
Melverley Church

NAVE   CHANCEL

Doorways and masonry styles can help to date the different parts of old churches, but usually the windows are the best evidence, although it should be remembered that windows were often inserted in older walling and occasionally dismantled and re-assembled within later walls. During the 12th century windows were gradually enlarged from the small round-headed windows of the 11th century to the long lancets with pointed heads which appeared c1200. A few late 12th century windows have external side-shafts, as at Condover and Edstaston. Before the mid 13th century two-light windows only occur in the belfry stages of towers, as at Eaton-under-Haywood, Linley and Much Wenlock. The earliest twinned lancets not in towers are at Cheswardine and Longford, both of which have chancel-chapels with five-light east windows. The room over the porch of c1250 at Shifnal has a window with two lights with a trefoil above, the earliest Shropshire example of plate tracery. Of the 1270s are two-light windows with trefoils above at Tugford and three and four light windows with circles containing quatrefoils and trefoils at Acton Burnell, where there are also single lancets with cusped heads in the sidewalls of the nave and chancel. At Alberbury and Atcham there are two-light windows where the mullion branches into two at the top to produce Y-tracery.

With the arrival of more complex and sometimes even perverse forms c1300 the Decorated style arrived. At Bitterley are windows of c1300-10 with three cusped lancets under a single head. East windows of c1310-20 at Much Wenlock, Munslow and Shifnal have three lancets with arch heads standing on their heads and another arch on top. Of the same period are those at Chelmarsh, Kinlet, Pontesbury and Stottesdon with intersecting tracery developed from the simple Y-tracery with the pattern broken at the top by a six-foiled or quatrefoiled circle, or, as at Edstaston, a spheric triangle. Spheric triangles without lancets below occur at Alberbury, Morton Corbet and St Mary's at Shrewsbury. Reticulation or net-like tracery occurs from c1330 onwards, as at Albrighton. The floral shapes at Claverley and the spikey stars at Worfield are perhaps of c1340.

The Perpendicular style was introduced into Shropshire with the remodelling of the abbey church at Shrewsbury in the 1360s. The west window has seven lights with secondary arches over groups of three but with the mullions nevertheless carrying straight up to the main arch , and the whole upper half filled with many cusped lights to give an overall impression of a rectangular grid. This is much more complex than anything in the parish churches, amongst which the which the next buildings to take up the style are the collegiate Battlefield of c1406-9 and Tong of c1410-15. Battlefield still has reticulated tracery alongside the newer forms. Windows of c1430-70 at Loppington and Ludlow illustrate the next development, with flatter four-centred heads and limited tracery, and many towers continue this style. By the early 16th century flat or nearly flat heads are the norm, with the lights merely cusped at the top and no tracery, as at Child's Ercall and Ditton Priors. The windows of c1515 at Tong are even more austere, lacking even cusps.

Elizabethan windows at Langley and Shipton have tracery which imitates forms of c1300. Loughton and More have early 17th century windows with round arches over the lights, but the nave of the 1660s at Condover has late 15th century style square-headed windows, a case of Gothic Survival. At Minsterley in the 1680s classical style windows were introduced. They are large, simple round-headed openings with a keystone in the arch and a projecting level sill. The same style windows appear in most of the 18th century churches. The Victorians experimented with all the medieval styles and examples of their era occur frequently in the churches they remodelled, enlarged or restored.

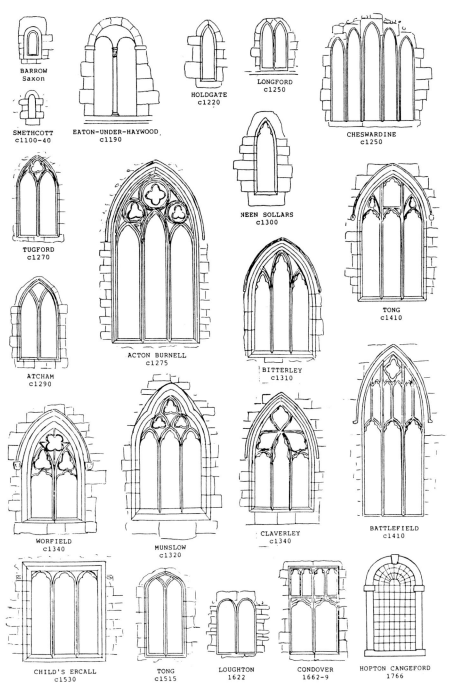

The development of church windows in Shropshire

Interior of Bromfield Church

Plain round fonts of c1130-1200 are common, having often survived later rebuilding of the church of that era, and there are two with boldly carved decoration of the middle of the 12th century at Holdgate and Stottesdon. That at Bucknell is one of the very few that may be earlier. Most of the octagonal later medieval fonts are fairly plain. Of greater interest is the font of c1280 on side-shafts at Acton Burnell, and the 15th century font at Ellesmere carved with the Instruments of Christ's Passion. A number of new fonts were made in the 1660s, that at Hodnet appearing to be in imitation Norman style, and that at Oswestry imitation 15th century.

Miserichord seat at Ludlow

Interior of Stokesay Church

It was the custom for the chancels of churches to be divided off from the nave by a screen to emphasise the greater sanctity of the east end. The screens became known as rood screens from the Holy Rood or image of the Crucifixion often mounted upon them. Sometimes there was a loft over the screen for the use of musicians and the performers of religious plays. Many rood screens and their lofts were ripped out during the Reformation of the mid 16th century and others were removed or cut down to the dado (the solid lower part) when their churches were restored in the 19th century. Stairs in the outer wall which gave access to the loft sometimes remain as a reminder of a long-lost screen and loft. Of about a dozen medieval rood screens now remaining in Shropshire the mid 14th century example at Hughley is the earliest. There are examples of note at Bettws-y-Crwyn and Ludlow, and one of the 17th century at Worthen. There are chapel screens of the 15th and 17th centuries respectively at Adderley and Ellesmere, and an aisle screen at Cleobury North.

Medieval pulpits are rare as long sermons only became fashionable in the 16th century. In Shropshire there are no pulpits earlier than the few of Elizabeth I's reign, but there are many of c1610-40, some with considerable ornamentation, usually quaint and rustic. A few medieval doors remain, but more common is the re-use of old ironwork on a more recent door. Some churches have altar rails of the late 16th, 17th and 18th century, but none of special importance. Bitterley and Neenton have the best of several examples of iron-bound medieval chests used to keep safe the church plate. The churches at Ludlow and Tong have 15th century stalls with miserichords (seats with lips to give a person support when standing), upon which are intersecting carved scenes. Over a dozen churches have medieval glass, but except for 14th century glass at St Mary's at Shrewsbury and 15th century glass at Ludlow it is all small fragments, often reset, and some of it is Continental glass brought over to England by rich travellers in the 19th century.

Brass at Harley

Tomb of St John Blount, d1531, at Kinlet

There are ten engraved brasses, ten incised alabaster slabs inlaid with pitch, three wooden effigies, and over two dozen stone and alabaster effigies earlier than c1540 in the churches of Shropshire. Tong has by far the best collection, with the earliest incised slab, three brasses and four fine 15th and 16th century effigies of knights and their ladies. Burford, Acton Burnell and Ightfield each have single notable brasses, whilst Berrington and Pitchford each have wooden 13th century effigies of knights. Eaton-under-Haywood has a rare 14th century wooden effigy of a man in civilian dress. Pitchford also has incised slabs of 1529 and 1534. Other notable monuments are the 13th century heraldic tomb at Albrighton, the 14th century coffin lids with foliated crosses and male figures at Preston Gubbals and Shrewsbury Abbey, the latter also having four effigies of the early and late 14th century. There is an effigy of c1320 at High Ercall, and there are effigies of the 15th and early 16th centuries at Burford, Kinlet, Moreton Corbet, Newport, Shifnall and Whitchurch.

Incised slab at Pitchford

Effigy at Neen Sollars

Pulpit at Minsterley

Waties monument at Ludlow   *Sundial at Edgmond*

Monuments of the period 1540-1700in Shropshire churches are more numerous than before, although there are only four brasses, none of great merit; and two incised slabs each at Claverley and Pitchford. There are 16th century tomb chests with recumbent effigies in the medieval manner but also with classical style decoration at Albrighton, Claverley, Moreton Corbet, Shrewsbury Abbey, Stoke-upon-Tern and Wroxeter. There are tombs of this type as late as 1637 and 1697 at Ludlow and Ludford respectively. Those of c1590 at Acton Burnell, Condover and Worfield are placed against a deep round or four-centred arch let into the church wall. The monument of 1632 at Acton Burnell is one of the best and latest of many monuments where modestly sized figures of a husband and wife kneel facing each other across a prayer desk. At Cardington, Ludlow and Neen Sollars there are fine early 17th century effigies in a semi-reclining attitude with a cheek resting on one hand and an elbow propped on the chest lid. At Aston Botterell, Kinlet and Worfield are large monuments with six posts supporting canopies above reclining figures, whilst Tong has a two-tier monument of 1632 with eight columns supporting the top tier. Rarest of all is the painted triptych of 1568 at Burford.

After 1640 effigies of the deceased became unusual and hanging tablets on the walls were favoured. Some are quite large and elaborate, with urns, cherubs and death symbols. Evidence of the early iron-making industry of Coalbrookdale are the cast-iron memorial slabs dating from the late 17th and early 18th centuries at Bridgnorth, Leighton and Onibury.

GAZETTEER OF SHROPSHIRE CHURCHES

ABDON   *St Margaret*   SO 575866

The church lies high up on the west slope of the Brown Clee Hill. Both nave and chancel are 14th century with a south doorway and one window of that date. The porch, the western part of the nave and the other windows are 19th century. Inside are four posts carrying a tiebeam to create a sort of tripartite chancel arch.

ACTON BURNELL   *St Mary*   SJ 534019

This fine church was built c1270-89 by Robert Burnell, Bishop of Bath and Wells and Lord Chancellor under Edward I. Both it and the adjacent embattled house which Burnell was licensed to crenellate in 1284 reflect his ability to obtain the best craftsmen of his time. The church is cruciform with transepts and a north porch adjoining the nave. The architectural features are original except for the small tower of 1887-9 tucked into the NE corner, and the roofs of 1571 and 1598 with arch-braced collars over the nave and chancel. All the windows are cusped lancets except for those in the four end walls. The west window just has three stepped lights but the other three additionally have stepped circles with and without foils. The chancel lancets are close grouped internally with only Purbeck marble shafts between them. The chancel has in the north wall a "leper's squint". Both the chancel and south transept have double piscinas, and the nave and transepts have corbel tables outside.

Notable furnishings are the font of c1280 with eight filletted shafts carrying trefoiled arches and the Jacobean pulpit. Grouped in the north transept are a tomb chest with an engraved brass of Sir Nicholas Burnell, d1382, recumbent effigies of Sir Richard Lee, d1591, and his wife on an elaborate alabaster tomb, and kneeling figures of Sir Humphrey Lee, d1632 and his wife. The latter were carved by Nicholas Stone and cost nearly £67. In the south transept is an ogival-headed 14th century tomb recess, now lacking an effigy.

Acton Burnell Church

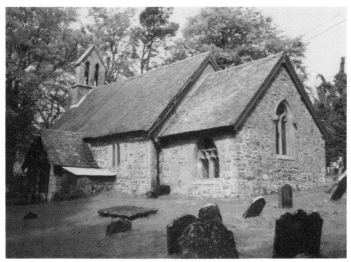

Abdon Church

Brass at Acton Burnell

ACTON ROUND   *Dedication unknown*   SO 635956

The nave masonry and south door ironwork are probably 12th century, and the south doorway and west window are 15th century. The porch is dated 1670 but may incorporate older parts. The north chapel is of the period of the monument it contains by Pritchard to Sir Whitmore Acton, d1731, and his wife, d1759. The thinly walled chancel with an ogee-headed priest's doorway is roughly contemporary. Inside it are half-figures of Richard Acton, d1703, and his wife.

ACTON SCOTT   *St Margaret*   SO 454894

The chief features of interest are the brass plate with kneeling figures of Thomas Mytton, d1577, and his family, and the monument to Edward Acton, d1747, designed by William Baker and executed by William Hiorns in 1751. The chancel and nave south wall are a 19th century rebuilding but the nave north wall is partly Norman, the west tower is perhaps 14th century, the south porch is dated 1722, and the Stackhouse Chapel on the north side is of c1820.

Font at Acton Burnell

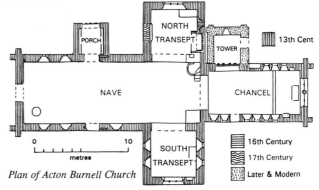

Plan of Acton Burnell Church

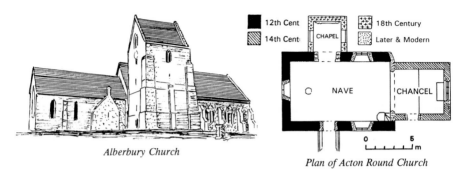

| 12th Cent | | 18th Century |
| 14th Cent | CHAPEL | Later & Modern |

Alberbury Church

Plan of Acton Round Church

ADDERLEY   *St Peter*   SJ 661395

Of the medieval church there survives only the square Norman font bearing rosettes and a curious later inscription. The church is of 1801 but there is a west tower of 1712-13 with large corner pilasters, a parapet obelisks and belfry windows with Y-tracery. On the north side is the Gothic Kilmorey Chapel of 1635-7. Over it the Corbets of Adderley and Lord Kilmorey of Shavington had a bitter quarrel. In one incident Sir John Corbet insulted the Kilmoreys by having his Irish foot boy buried without a coffin over the body of the late Lady Kilmory, but the Earl Marshal ordered the boy's body removed. The chapel and eastern part of the church are maintained by the Redundant Churches fund since they are no longer used on a regular basis. Inside this part lie a classical screen and brasses of Sir Robert Needham, d1560, and his family, and a late 14th century ecclesiastic. See page 26.

Brass at Adderley

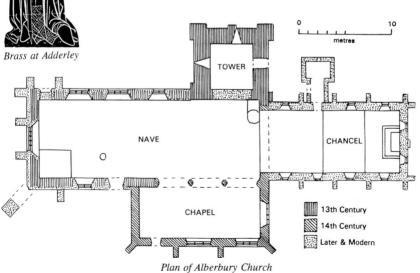

| 13th Century |
| 14th Century |
| Later & Modern |

Plan of Alberbury Church

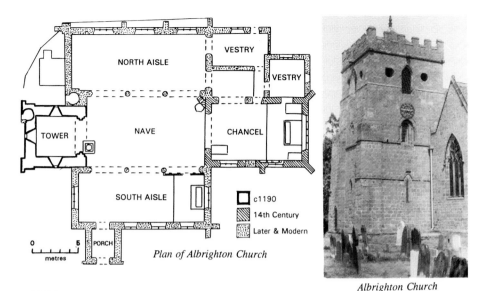

Plan of Albrighton Church

c1190

14th Century

Later & Modern

Albrighton Church

ALBERBURY   *St Michael*   SJ 358144

Nothing remains of a Saxon collegiate church at Alberbury. The earliest parts of the present church alongside the castle ruins are the nave and north tower of the 1290s. The tower was so placed so that it did not overlook the castle courtyard and it has clasping buttresses, lancets and windows with cusped Y-tracery. The nave was refaced externally in 1902 but it retains a fine old roof of collar-beams on arched braces forming semi-circles, with five tiers of wind-braces. The present chancel is of 1845 but the chancel arch and the three bay Loton Chapel on the south side of the nave are of c1320-30. The earliest of two large hanging monuments to Lysters of Rowton Castle, who died in 1691 and 1766, formerly lay in old St Chad's at Shrewsbury. There is also a monument to Dorothy Leighton, d1688.

ALBRIGHTON   *St John the Baptist*   SJ 497180

The neo-Norman church of 1840-1 contains a genuine round Norman font decorated with a nailhead motif plus beaded chevrons and petals. There is a plain Jacobean pulpit with a tester or sounding board above it.

ALBRIGHTON   *St Mary Magdalene*   SJ 809044

Albrighton was a borough from 1303 to 1834 but the church only attained town size in 1853 when the present aisles were erected and an organ chamber and a second vestry were added. The Late Norman west tower has clasping corner buttresses and round-headed belfry windows but the lancet windows below have the more advanced pointed heads. The tower arch is of c1300 and the battlements are even later. The 14th century chancel has windows with reticulated tracery on the south, and a transomed five-light east window. A vestry of ancient but uncertain date adjoins it on the NE. Beside the altar are the defaced effigies of Sir John Talbot, d1555, and his wife, and a plain tomb chest, probably of the only Duke of Shrewsbury, d1718. The heraldic tomb chest without an effigy was discovered under the floor in 1853. It may be that of Andrew Fitz-Nicholas of Willey, killed in battle at Evesham in 1265.

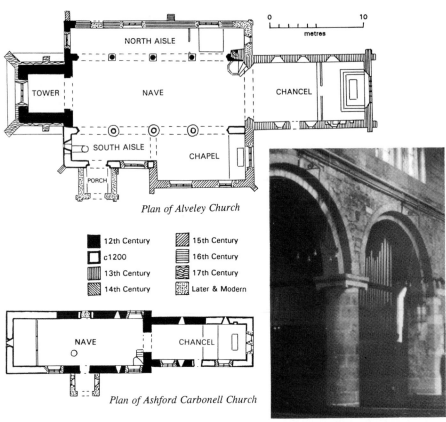

Plan of Alveley Church

■ 12th Century	▨ 15th Century
☐ c1200	▤ 16th Century
▦ 13th Century	▧ 17th Century
▩ 14th Century	▨ Later & Modern

Plan of Ashford Carbonell Church

Alveley Church

ALVELEY   *St Mary*   SO 759845

Although heavily restored by Sir Arthur Blomfield in 1878-9, this church is an interesting composite of various periods. The tower was refaced and buttressed in the 17th century and given a new top in 1779, but is essentially Norman, with a moulded round arch with nook-shafts. The four bay north arcade of c1190 has round piers with leaf capitals and pointed arches. Most of the aisle walling was rebuilt in 1585, that year and the name Jhon Dauis, Freemason, appearing in the blocked north doorway. The south arcade, aisle, and doorway are early 13th century. The eastern part of the aisle was later widened to form the Coton Chapel, endowed in 1353 as a chantry chapel. The features of the 13th century chancel were all renewed in 1878-9. In the north aisle is a late 15th century silk altar frontal depicting Abraham with souls in his bosom and cherubs on either side. On the floor by the tower is a brass to John Grove, who endowed the local school and died in 1616.

ASHFORD BOWDLER   *St Andrew*   SO 519705

Two tiny Norman windows remain in the chancel, which is set right by the River Teme. The two Norman nave doorways were blocked up in the 14th century when a western extension with a new south doorway was constructed. The church was restored in 1853 and 1871.

ASHFORD CARBONELL   *St Mary*   SO 525710

The original Norman nave and chancel, divided by a small and plain round arch, were in the late 12th century given a new north doorway with dogtooth on the hoodmould, and extensions at either end, thus producing a long, narrow building. The vesica window over two small round-headed lancets in the east wall is mostly a 19th century reconstruction. Several genuine 12th century windows remain in the side walls, plus others of the 14th and 15th centuries. The nave roof is old, with tie-beams, hammer-beams, and arch-braced collar-beams. Perched on one tie-beam is a pyramidal-roofed timber belfry.

ASTLEY   *St Mary*   SJ 530188

The nave has a wide blocked late 12th century south doorway with stiff-leaf decoration on the capitals of the nook-shafts. Another Norman doorway opens into the chancel, but above the lowest courses much of the church is 14th century, with two 16th century windows, a west tower of 1837, and much restoration of 1887.

ASTLEY ABBOTS   *St Calixtus*   SO 709962

Of the church consecrated in 1138 there remains the north wall of the nave with two windows and a blocked doorway. On the east gable of the very wide chancel is the date 1633, when the church was rebuilt and widened. The priest's doorway is round-headed but the east window (which contains some glass of c1300) is Gothic. Also of the 1630s are the pulpit, the panelling in the chancel, and the hammerbeam-roof supported on stone animal corbels. In 1857 the south wall and porch were rebuilt and the west wall given internal and external buttressing to support a small tower. The "Maiden's Garland" dated 1707 is an unusual relic (but see also Minsterley).

ASTON BOTTERELL   *St Michael*   SO 633841

Of the 12th century are the font and the nave and chancel of equal width with one original window in the latter. The south aisle with a low three bay arcade on round piers was added in the 13th century, as was the west tower, although only the tower arch survived a rebuilding in 1884. The east window and buttresses are 15th century, the porch is dated 1639, and three north windows are Victorian. The nave has an old roof with tie-beams and wind-braces. An incised slab depicts John Botterell, d1479, and his wife, and an elaborate tomb in the aisle has effigies of John Botterell, d1588, and his wife Elizabeth.

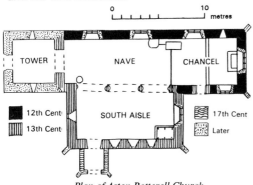

Plan of Aston Botterell Church   *Aston Botterell Church*

ASTON EYRE   *Dedication Unknown*   SO 653941

The nave is probably that built by Robert Fitz Aer in 1135-40, but the pointed chancel arch and thinly walled chancel may be slightly later. The chancel has two 13th century windows in the side walls but there are no other alterations apart from some windows being renewed. There is a fine tympanum over the south doorway depicting Christ's entry into Jerusalem. He faces the front and is seated on an ass. On his right an old man spreads palm branches for the ass to step on and to the left is another man with an ass.

ASTON HALL   *No Dedication Recorded*   SJ 325271

By the hall is a red brick chapel of 1742 with a west tower with angle pilasters. The nave and chancel window tracery is Victorian.

ATCHAM   *St Eata*   SJ 542092

The early 13th century tower is probably built of Roman stones from Wroxeter. It has a deep round-arched west portal with several orders of shafts facing the adjacent River Severn, and broad, flat corner buttresses. The 12th century nave is thinly walled considering its great width. One original round-headed window in the north wall has a triangular rere-arch. Two other nave windows are 15th century insertions. At the end of the 13th century the Norman chancel was replaced by a new one the same width as the nave with Y-traceried side-windows. Some windows contain 15th and 16th century glass brought here in 1811 from the church at Bacton in Herefordshire. The east window contains the kneeling family of Miles ap Parry, c1490, and a north window contains figures of Elizabeth I and her gentlewoman Blanche Parry, d1589, shown kneeling at the queen's feet presenting a book. On the south wall is an incised alabaster slab formerly in old St Chad's at Shrewsbury. It depicts Edward Burton of Longnor Hall, d1524, and his wife Joyce with seven daughters. The timber south porch is dated 1685.

BADGER   *St Giles*   SO 768997

The thin tower and the main body of the church date from 1834 and the porch and north chapel are additions of 1886, but the very low round tower arch must be Norman, and there are roundels of 16th or 17th century glass from the Netherlands in the east window.

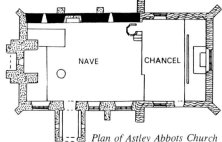

Plan of Astley Abbots Church

0   10

metres

▥ Saxon

■ 12th Century

▦ 13th Century

▧ 15th Century

▨ 17th Century

▩ Later & Modern

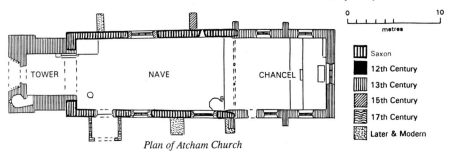

Plan of Atcham Church

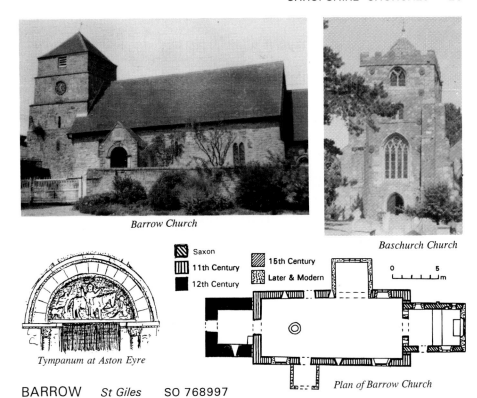

Barrow Church

Baschurch Church

Saxon
11th Century
12th Century

15th Century
Later & Modern

Tympanum at Aston Eyre

Plan of Barrow Church

BARROW   *St Giles*   SO 768997

This is a church of great architectural interest. The chancel is clearly Saxon and possibly once formed a self-contained chapel. In the middle of its north wall there are signs of a former pilaster strip and there is also a small double-splayed window. The chancel arch has a square hoodmould which may have originally gone down to the ground beside the imposts. It is later than the chancel, but possibly earlier than the mid to late 11th century nave. The nave has original doorways to the north, south and west, the last being tall and having a tympanum decorated with three tiers of lozenges and saltire crosses. It now looks into the base of an early 12th century tower of three stages, each smaller than that below. The brick top and pyramidal roof are much later. The nave had three Norman round-headed windows on each side but three of the six have been replaced by larger windows of the 13th, 15th and 19th centuries. The brick south porch is dated 1705. The north transept bears the date 1688 and contains 18th century monuments, but appears to have been entirely rebuilt in the 19th century.

BASCHURCH   *All Saints*   SJ 422218

The nave north wall and the whole of the short chancel were rebuilt in 1790, whilst the Late Norman six-bay arcade with round piers, square abaci and round arches was mostly renewed in 1894, along with several other features. The wide south aisle with several tomb recesses on the inner side dates from the early 14th century. Outside there are traces of a former two storey porch. The tower is 13th century with 15th century buttresses. There is a Rococo monument to William Basnett, d1754.

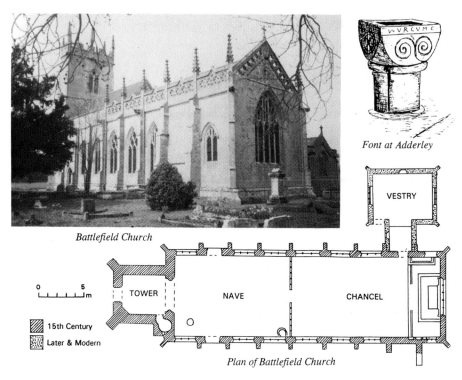

Font at Adderley

Battlefield Church

0 5m

15th Century

Later & Modern

TOWER NAVE CHANCEL

VESTRY

Plan of Battlefield Church

BATTLEFIELD   *St Mary Magdalene*   SJ 512173

After his defeat of Hotspur Percy here in 1403, Henry IV showed his gratitude by building a new church with a college of eight chaplains to pray for the souls of those slain. The wide nave and chancel are divided only by a screen. The tower was added slightly later. Money for the tower was collected in 1429, but it was not completed until the time of Master Adam Grafton (1478-1520), who set his own name upon it. The church superseded that of Albright Hussey, which eventually disappeared. The church at Battlefield was itself neglected during the 18th century when there were few parishioners to support it, but it was restored by S. Pountney Smith in 1861. From that period date the parapets, pinnacles, north vestry, the statue of Henry IV on the east gable, and the roofs, the present nave roof having a higher aspect than the original. In the vestry is some 16th century glass from Normandy, and in the chancel is a 15th century statue of the Madonna Pieta holding the dead Christ. Nothing remains of the college buildings to the south, although there are remains of the moat which surrounded the precinct.

BECKBURY   *St Milburga*   SJ 765015

The chancel is of c1300 and has a shallow, later tomb recess, now refaced, in the outside of the north wall. The same wall inside bears a incised slab depicting Roger Houghton, d1505, in armour and his family. A new nave and small tower with a doorway with alternating rustication were added in the 1730s, a three bay south aisle and a north chapel were added in 1856, the remainder of the north aisle was built in 1879, and the timber north porch was added in 1887.

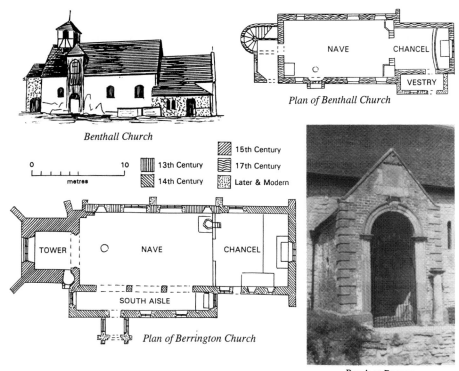

Benthall Church

Plan of Benthall Church

▨ 15th Century		
▥ 13th Century	▩ 17th Century	
▧ 14th Century	▨ Later & Modern	

0 ————— 10
metres

Plan of Berrington Church

Porch at Barrow

BEDSTONE   *St Mary*   SO 368758

The nave and chancel, separated by a plain round arch, are Norman, and each has one original window. All the other features are Victorian.

BENTHALL   *St Bartholomew*   SO 657025

The medieval chapel of St Brice was badly damaged during the Civil War, when the adjacent hall was garrisoned by each side in turn. The existing nave and chancel, of interest but not handsome, date entirely from the rebuilding of 1667 recorded on the gallery. In 1884-7 and 1892-3 the vestry, west porch and apsidal gallery access stair projection were added and the three-decker pulpit in the middle of the south wall removed (the new pulpit was made from its materials). The roofs are of 1667. Of the 18th century are the box pews, the rector's pew, squire's pew, and the monument to Ralph Brown, d1707.

BERRINGTON   *All Saints*   SJ 530069

The oldest feature is the round 12th century font with seven heads, an animal, a cock, and a candle. The 13th century nave north wall has one original lancet window. Otherwise the wide, undivided nave and chancel with original roofs and the narrow three bay south aisle are all of the 14th century. The west tower is 15th century and most of the windows are 19th century, as is the south porch, except for its outer entrance, which is the original 13th century doorway reset. In the south aisle is a late 13th century oak effigy of a cross-legged knight.

BERWICK   *No Dedication Recorded*   SJ 473148

In the grounds of Berwick House is a little-used chapel of 1672 with plain mullion and transom windows and original box-pews, pulpit and west gallery. The west tower is probably of the 1730s, and the east end and transepts were added in 1892-4.

BETTWS-Y-CRWYN   *St Mary*   SO 206814

This church lies high up in a very remote position. The chancel, porch and all of the windows are of 1860, but the nave masonry is probably 13th century and there is a fine old roof with collar-beams on arched braces and three tiers of wind-braces. Inside is a late medieval screen with round arches, intricate panel tracery, and a frieze of pierced quatrefoils above the dado.

BICTON   *No Dedication Recorded*   SJ 704854

Bicton was a chapelry of St Chad at Shrewsbury until made a parish in 1853. It has a ruined 18th century church, disused since Holy Trinity church was built some way to the SE in 1886.

BILLINGSLEY   *St Mary*   SO 704854

The Norman south doorway was blocked later on in the 12th century when a western extension was added with a new south doorway with nook-shafts and a thick roll-moulded arch and a tympanum with hatched triangles. Also Norman is the font. The chancel is 14th century and has an Easter Sepulchre on the north side, but was externally refaced in the 19th century. The timber south porch is of c1500 and the pulpit and reader's desk are of the 17th century.

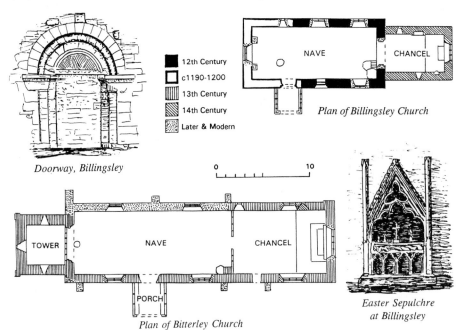

■ 12th Century
☐ c1190-1200
▥ 13th Century
▨ 14th Century
▦ Later & Modern

Doorway, Billingsley

NAVE   CHANCEL

Plan of Billingsley Church

0   10

TOWER   NAVE   CHANCEL

PORCH

Plan of Bitterley Church

Easter Sepulchre at Billingsley

BISHOP'S CASTLE

St John the Baptist   SO 324884

A large new aisled nave and polygonal apse were built in 1860 to a design by Thomas Nicholson. Of the old church there survive only the low west tower and part of a 16th century monument, and some reset architectural fragments in the vicarage garden wall. The tower may originally have been Norman, but the battlements and possibly the whole structure may be of the restoration of 1662 after the medieval church was severely damaged during the Civil War of the 1640s.

Bishop's Castle Church

BITTERLEY   *St Mary*   SO 570774

The west tower and the nave and chancel, which are undivided except by a 19th century screen, are mostly of the 13th century. Part of the south wall might be older, there are several windows of c1300-20, and the east window and entire nave north wall are of 1876 and 1880. The Norman font has round arches, and there are a Jacobean pulpit and a long 13th century iron-bound chest. An effigy of Timothy Lucy, d1616, in armour, lies in the chancel, and there are many tablets to members of the Powys, Pardoe and Walcot families. The bells are interesting, the tenor of 1414 having an inscription in Norman-French, and others of 1450 and 1510 having Latin inscriptions. The 14th century churchyard cross has a hexagonal shaft and a Crucifixion is still visible on the west face of the very weathered head. See p8.

BONINGALE   *St Chad*   SJ 812026

The small Norman nave and chancel each have an original window and the chancel has lancets of the 14th and 15th centuries. The south aisle, west wall, weatherboarded belfry, chancel arch, vestry, and north windows are all of 1861. Inside is a Jacobean pulpit.

BORASTON   *Dedication Unknown*   SO 614700

Two blocked doorways and some walling are Norman, other parts with one window are of c1300, and inside is a spiral-fluted font of c1700 transferred here from Buildwas. Everything else is of the restoration of 1884-7 by Henry Curzon.

BOURTON   *Holy Trinity*   SO 597964

Bourton was a chapel-of-ease to Much Wenlock. The nave and chancel are Norman but are overpowered by the north aisle and inserted windows of 1844. The south porch is of uncertain date. Inside are a Norman font and Jacobean pews, reader's desk and pulpit.

St Mary Magdalene's Church, Bridgnorth

St Leonard's Church, Bridgnorth

BRIDGNORTH   *St Leonard*   SO 717934

The church has a fine situation in a close of old buildings which opens out to give a vista of the River Severn far below to the east. It is an exceptionally wide building mostly dating from the restoration of 1860-2, but the south tower of 1870 is a replica of that built by Richard Horde in 1448, some medieval masonry may survive in the south aisle, and the chancel has a 14th century north wall with a leper's squint. The nave hammerbeam roof is of 1662. By the 1530s there were seven chantries in this church, which was declared redundant in 1978, since when all services have been held at St Mary Magdalene at the other end of the town. In the south aisle are several cast-iron tombstones of between 1679 and 1707, brought inside from the graveyard.

BRIDGNORTH   *St Mary Magdalene*   SO 717928

The original medieval chapel of the castle of Bridgnorth was in 1792 replaced by a splendid new classical style church designed by Thomas Telford. The church is orientated south-north so that the ritual west tower actually faces northwards down the length of East Castle Street, which was originally part of the castle outer bailey. The tower rises above a facade with giant Tuscan columns, rustication and a pediment, and has a circular porch in its base. The tall bell-stage has Tuscan columns and is surmounted by an octagonal clock-stage and a lead dome. The main body of the church has couple Doris pilasters and tall arched windows. Originally there was a straight east end but in 1876 Arthur Blomfield added an apse. The arcades inside have a straight entablature carried on huge fluted Ionic columns.

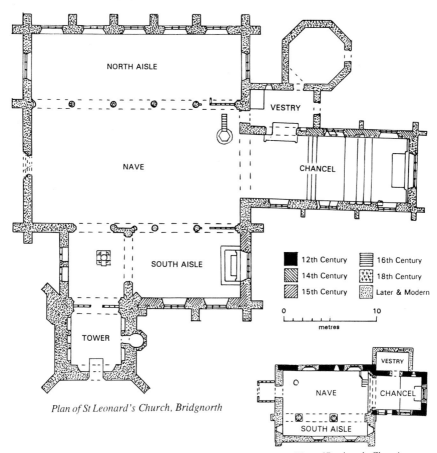

Plan of St Leonard's Church, Bridgnorth

12th Century   16th Century
14th Century   18th Century
15th Century   Later & Modern

0   10
metres

Plan of Boningale Church

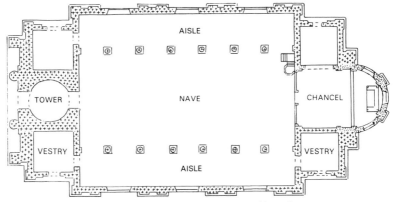

Plan of St Mary Magdalene's Church, Bridgnorth

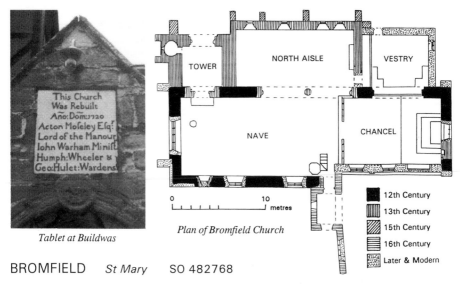

This Church
Was Rebuilt
Año:Dom:1720
Acton Moseley Esqr
Lord of the Manour
John Warham Minist.
Humph:Wheeler &
Geo:Hulet:Wardens

Tablet at Buildwas

Plan of Bromfield Church

0   10
|_____| metres

■ 12th Century
▦ 13th Century
▨ 15th Century
▤ 16th Century
▩ Later & Modern

BROMFIELD   *St Mary*   SO 482768

Bromfield had a collegiate church which is mentioned in the Domesday Book of 1086. It was made into a Benedictine priory in 1135, affiliated to Gloucester Abbey. Of a cruciform church of about that period there remain the east and north arches of the central tower and the masonry of the nave. At the end of the 13th century a wide north aisle with a two bay arcade and a NW porch-tower were added, but the inner doorway is slightly earlier. At the Dissolution of the monasteries the chancel was taken down and the south transept was replaced by a house built by Charles Foxe, the old central tower then becoming part of the house. Ruins of parts of the house still remain but most of it was removed in 1658 and the old crossing space then became the chancel of the church. This part was given a painted ceiling by Thomas Francis in 1672. Except for the fine recess of c1330, the chancel south wall, the vestry on the site of the north transept and the nave windows are all of 1879. Of the priory buildings there remain only the 14th century gateway with a timber framed upper storey set on a stone basement. See pictures on cover and page 14.

BROUGHTON   *St Mary*   SJ 501239

In a field near the former Yorton Station are two low ivy-clad walls of the late 12th century chancel of the old church which was abandoned because of damp. A pyx of c1500 is in the new church of 1858 to the south.

BUCKNELL   *St Mary*   SO 355739

The 11th century font has an interlace pattern on the bowl. The nave masonry is also Norman and the chancel is 14th century with an original priest's doorway and south window, but the north aisle, vestry and all the other features are of 1870.

BUILDWAS   *Holy Trinity*   SJ 637047

The nave and the south porch are of 1720, the year appearing on an iron plate on the porch. Earlier only is the Jacobean pulpit. The chancel, vestry and timber-framed belfry are of 1864.

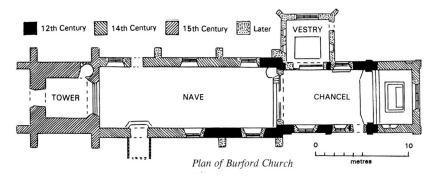

Plan of Burford Church

BURFORD *St Mary* SO 584680

The church is long since the 12th century building was extended at either end in the 14th century and given a west tower in the 15th century. Norman masonry with pilaster buttresses survives in the western two bays of the chancel and the east bay of the nave. The vestry is of 1860 and the chancel arch and tower top are of 1889. The church has a 15th century panelled font and many fine monuments. Beside the altar is a life-sized brass to Elizabeth de Cornwayle, d1370. The alabaster effigy under an arch in the chancel north wall is of Elizabeth, sister of Henry IV, who married firstly John Holland, Earl of Huntingdon and Duke of Exeter, and secondly Sir John Cornwayle, Lord Stanhope. She died in 1426. The wooden figure of a man in plate armour in the middle of the chancel is Edmund Cornwall, d1508, aged only 20. A very rare monument is the lofty painted triptych signed and dated Melchior Salabuss, 1588, with portraits of Richard Cornwall, d1568, and his parents. Two other memorials of 1630 each show couples kneeling facing each other.

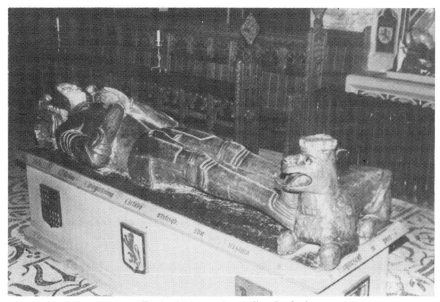

Tomb of Edmund Cornwall at Burford

BURWARTON   *St Laurence*   SO 617849

Below the church of 1877, now sold off for private use, are ruins of a Norman church with a round chancel arch. The west wall has gone and the east wall is 18th century. One window is 14th century.

CARDESTON   *St Michael*   SO 506952

Apart from a Norman window in the chancel the church is of 1749. New windows and a west tower with an octagonal upper storey were added in 1844. In the tower is a chest dated 1703.

CARDINGTON   *St James*   SO 506952

This is a long church with a 12th century nave extended westward later in that century and a 13th century west tower and chancel, all three parts having the same width externally. The nave extension has new north and south doorways superseding those further east. The chancel was re-windowed c1300 and the nave gained new windows in the 14th century, whilst the tower was given a new arch and a top stage in the 15th century. The south porch is of 1639, and the chancel arch and east window are of 1867. The chancel has a fine old roof. The Jacobean pulpit has carvings of mermen. On the south side of the chancel is a fine monument to William Leighton of Plaish, Chief Justice of Wales, d1607 and his wife and children. One child died as an infant and is shown leaning against a skull. The south door bears the initials of Richard Corfield and the year 1648.

Doorway at Child's Ercall

CAYNHAM   *St Mary*   SO 554733

All that survives the rebuilding by James Brookes in 1885 is part of the west tower of c1200 and the slightly earlier south doorway and pointed chancel arch with contemporary side arches.

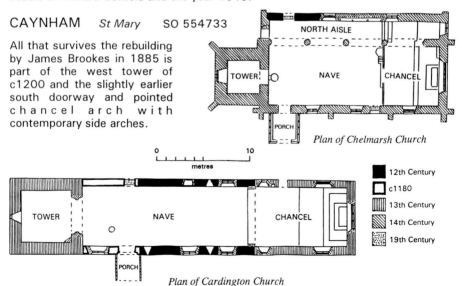

Plan of Chelmarsh Church

12th Century
c1180
13th Century
14th Century
19th Century

Plan of Cardington Church

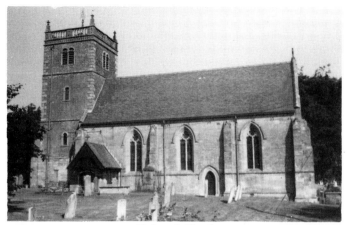

Chelmarsh Church

0   5
└─┴─┴─┴─┴─┘ m

CHELMARSH *St Peter* SO 721878

Plan of Burwarton Old Church

The nave and chancel of equal width and the four bay arcade with ballflowers on the capitals of the octagonal piers date from the years leading up to 1345, when Hugh Mortimer founded a chantry in the church. Some of the masonry, together with a blocked doorway, in the aisle is 12th century. The west tower of brick on a stone base is of c1700 but has a reset 14th century west window. Part of a 15th century tomb chest is now used as a credence table, and there are reused old parts in the screen and pulpit.

CHESWARDINE *St Swithin* SJ 719299

Carvings of the Talbot dog and Stafford knot below the tower belfry windows suggest it was built between 1467 and 1473. The 13th century north chapel has an east window composed of five lancets and contains a contemporary foliated coffin lid. The rest of the church is of 1888-9 by J.L.Pearson, but the round arched south arcade and pointed arched north arcade in the nave probably reflect former 12th and 13th century originals.

CHETTON *St Giles* SO 664904

The chancel is 13th century with several original windows and a priest's doorway, but the chancel arch is not much earlier than c1300 and rests on two primitive heads of c1500. The nave was rebuilt in 1788 and provided with new windows in 1891-2, and the west tower is of 1829.

CHILD'S ERCALL *St Michael* SJ 666251

The chancel and north aisle of 1879 have a reset late 12th century doorway and east window respectively, the round piers on the south being slightly earlier than the octagonal piers on the north. The south aisle was rebuilt wider in the early 14th century and the SW tower and west wall of the nave are of the early 16th century.

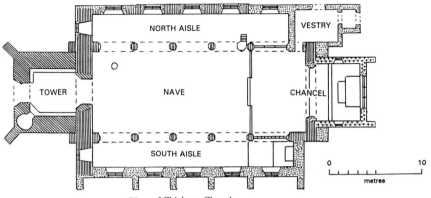

Plan of Chirbury Church

13th Century   18th Century
14th Century   Later & Modern

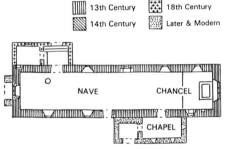

Plan of Church Preen Church

Interior of Church Stretton Church

CHIRBURY   *St Michael*   SO 262985

The five bay nave and aisles with pointed arches on circular piers date from after c1227 when an Augustinian priory was transferred to Chirbury from Snead. A short blue-brick chancel of 1733 replaces the eastern parts of the church which were destroyed in the 1540s. A massive west tower with inner and outer triple-chamfered arches was begun c1300 but the top parts are of the early 16th century. The NE vestry, chancel arch and aisle windows are of the restoration of 1871. The stalls and rood screen survive in a church over the Welsh border at Montgomery.

CHURCH PREEN   *St John the Baptist*   SO 543982

The church has a long narrow 13th century nave and chancel of equal width which originally served a monastic cell subservient to Wenlock Priory. Notable are the three east lancets of equal height and the transomed lancet in the north wall. The small embattled south chapel is of the 1920s, whilst there is an 18th century porch and adjoining vestry at the NW corner. The pulpit and reading desk are both of 1641.

CHURCH PULVERBATCH   *St Edith*   SJ 430030

Only a 15th century octagonal font and the west tower of 1733 with a circular west window and bell openings with Y-tracery survived the rebuilding of 1853.

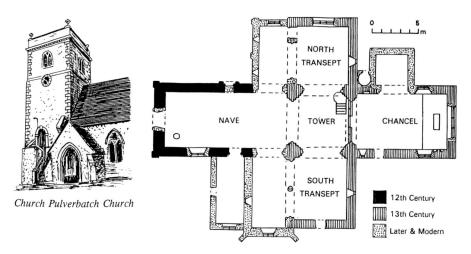

Church Pulverbatch Church

NORTH TRANSEPT

NAVE

TOWER

CHANCEL

SOUTH TRANSEPT

0   5
└─┴─┴─┴─┴─┘ m

■ 12th Century

▥ 13th Century

▨ Later & Modern

CHURCH STRETTON   *St Lawrence*   SO 453937

The Norman nave has corner pilaster buttresses and a north doorway with two rolls in the arch and a sheila-na-gig above, and a south doorway with one order of shafts. In the 13th century the building was made cruciform with a new central tower, chancel, and transepts, and the trussed rafter roof of the nave is also of this period. Between 1300 and 1340 various windows were inserted, whilst the east window appears to be of the 1630s. The village grew after the railway arrived and in 1867-83 the transepts were given western aisles and a vestry and organ loft were added. The font is 15th century and there is 16th and 17th century Flemish glass in the chancel windows. There is Jacobean woodwork around the font and behind the altar.

Church Stretton Church

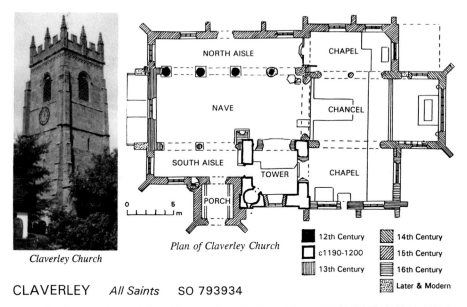

Claverley Church

Plan of Claverley Church

■ 12th Century	▨ 14th Century
□ c1190-1200	▨ 15th Century
▥ 13th Century	▤ 16th Century
	▦ Later & Modern

NORTH AISLE — CHAPEL — NAVE — CHANCEL — SOUTH AISLE — TOWER — CHAPEL — PORCH

0   5 m

CLAVERLEY   *All Saints*   SO 793934

Claverley has a substantial and interesting church with work from various periods. In 1902 foundations of a very small Saxon chancel were found at the west end of the present one and a remarkable series of wall-paintings of c1200 were re-exposed on the walling above the 12th century north arcade. The armed knights on horseback are thought to illustrate the Battle of the Virtues and Vices. The frieze was originally longer, for the western respond of the arcade is a whole pier, and a fifth bay appears to have been removed c1280 when the present west wall and south arcade of just two bays were built. The aisle walls, the south porch and the upper parts of the south transeptal tower are 15th century, but the lower part of the tower is of c1190 and one jamb of the original tower arch, buried in the masonry of a narrower 16th century arch, was revealed in 1902. The chancel with three sedilia and a piscina with ogival heads is 14th century, whilst the chancel arch and rood staircase, plus the north chapel with a two bay arcade are late 15th century. The 16th century south chapel has a single wide arch towards the chancel. The north chapel has fine windows of c1340 reset from the chancel north wall. A medieval NE vestry has been demolished.

The font is Norman and the pulpit is Jacobean. An incised slab to the merchant Richard Spicer, d1448, and his wife Alice lies in the north chapel. The south chapel contains the fine tomb of Sir Robert Broke of Ludstone Hall, Speaker of the House of Commons and Chief Justice of the Common Pleas, d1558, with effigies of him, two wives and sixteen children. On the chapel east wall are incised slabs to Francis Gatacre of Swyerton, d1599, and his wife Elizabeth, and Sir William Gatacre, d1577, and his wife Helen.

CLEE ST MARGARET   *St Margaret*   SO 565844

The late 12th century nave has an original door and doorway on the south and a very narrow plain pointed chancel arch with secondary opening on either side. The chancel itself has herringbone masonry and is likely to be of the 11th century. It has two Norman windows plus a 14th century one. The porch and vestry are 19th century, and the pulpit and benches are 17th century.

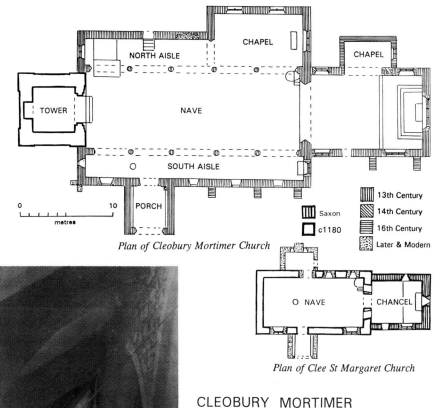

Plan of Cleobury Mortimer Church

▥	13th Century
▨	14th Century
▤	16th Century
▦	Later & Modern

▥ Saxon

☐ c1180

Plan of Clee St Margaret Church

Cleobury Mortimer Church

CLEOBURY MORTIMER

St Mary   SO 674757

Cleobury is a small town and has quite a large church. The tower has a horseshoe-shaped tower arch and is late 12th century with a 13th century top and a still later shingled broach-spire which was last renewed in 1898 and has since become twisted owing to warping of the timbers. The wide nave and chancel, the splendid chancel arch, and the narrow south aisle with a five bay arcade and large porch are all early to mid 13th century. The north aisle of c1290-1320 has two wider east bays forming the chapel of St Nicholas. Both nave and chancel have 14th century roofs, and the latter has 14th and 16th century windows and a small 16th century north chapel or vestry with a squint pointing towards the high altar. The south buttresses are Victorian. In the south aisle is an old chest. See photo on page 8.

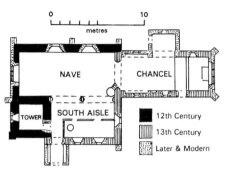

Arcade in Clun Church   *Plan of Cleobury North Church*

CLEOBURY NORTH   *St Peter and St Paul*   SO 624870

The nave is Norman and has a 13th century south aisle with a two bay arcade. At the west end of the aisle is a small SW tower of uncertain date with a later brick top. The narrow chancel is 13th century, but was heavily restored in 1890-1. The aisle windows and porch are probably of 1838. The aisle has an old roof and contains a 13th century font surrounded by a screen c1500 to create a squire's pew. The pulpit is dated 1628 and there is a contemporary double seat.

CLIVE   *All Saints*   SJ 515240

Most of the church, including the spectacular tower and spire, is of the rebuilding of 1885-94. Two Norman doorways survive, plus 12th and 15th century nave masonry visible on the outer south side.

Cleobury North Church   *Clun Church*

Doorway at Clun

CLUN *St George* SO 301805

The squat 12th century tower with a timber top storey and pyramidal roof backs onto the west wall of a wide Early Norman nave with the west window still surviving. The four bay arcades are Late Norman and have pointed arches on circular piers with scalloped capitals. In Street's restoration of 1877 a narrow new south aisle replaced a wider medieval one, the east end of the chancel was rebuilt, and the Early Norman arch now looking into the organ space and the eastern pier of each of arcade were renewed. The wide 13th century north aisle has renewed lancets. The tomb recess on the north side is 14th century and the two storey porch overlapping the NW corner may also be of that date. The nave and north aisle have 15th century roofs with collar-beams on arched braces with three tiers of quatrefoil wind-braces. A reredos at the north aisle east end and the pulpit and tester are 17th century.

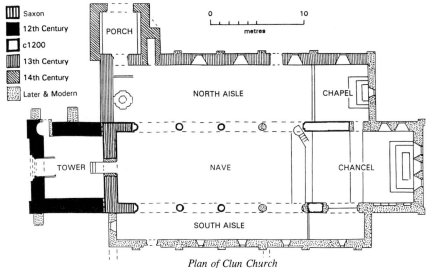

Plan of Clun Church

Clungunford Church

CLUNBURY   *St Swithun*   SO 371806

The original Norman church comprised the eastern two thirds of the nave, which has traces of a former doorway, and the chancel, with one original north window. The nave was lengthened westwards late in the 12th century and new south and west doorways then provided. The latter now opens into a short but massive early 13th century tower. The font is Late Norman, and there are several nave windows of the 14th and 15th centuries. The back remains of a Jacobean pulpit.

Transept at Condover

Plan of Cold Weston Church

CLUNGUNFORD   *St Cuthbert*   SO 395788

The long aisleless nave and chancel are both of c1300, but were restored in 1895 by E.Turner, who added the north tower and the south porch. The north chapel, with small pairs of lancets on the north side, may be slightly earlier than the rest of the church.

COLD WESTON   *St Mary*   SO 552830

This tiny Norman church lies high up on the slopes of the Titterstone Clee Hill and is reached across fields. The east window is dated 1719 but the other features are all of the 19th century.

COCKSHUTT   *St Helen*   SJ 434293

This brick church of 1777 was altered in 1886. It has a nave and apse with pointed-headed windows and a west tower with round-headed windows.

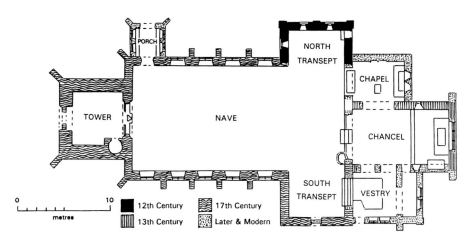

Plan of Condover Church

CONDOVER   *St Mary & St Andrew*   SJ 494058

The fine Late Norman north transept and some masonry of the 13th century chancel are all that predate the disaster of 1660, when, after alterations to the supporting piers, the central tower collapsed. In 1662-4 a new south transept, shorter than the old one, and a wide nave corresponding to the width of the Norman nave and the north aisle of c1300 were erected as a cost of £2,750. In 1670-9 a new west tower was built by John Orum, whose initials appear on the tower arch. All the details are still late medieval in style. The Cholmondley Chapel north of the chancel was added in 1867-8 and the vestry, north porch and nave buttresses were added during Fairfax Wade's restoration of 1878, when a plaster ceiling of c1790-1813 was removed to reveal the fine 17th century hammerbeam roof. There are recumbent alabaster effigies of Thomas Scriven, d1657, and his wife, a frontal bust of Martha Owen, d1641 (from old St Chad's at Shrewsbury), and in the Cholmondley Chapel are pairs of figures facing each other of Dame Jane Norton, d1640, her husband, her brother Sir Roger Owen, and her father Judge Owen, plus a figure by Roubiliac of Roger Owen, d1746.

CORELEY   *St Peter*   SO 613739

At the west end of the brick nave and chancel of 1757 is a short 13th century west tower. The porch, vestry and windows are all 19th century.

COUND   *St Peter*   SJ 558050

The north aisle, chancel and vestry are of 1841, 1862, and 1889-91 respectively. The south aisle and four bay arcade are 13th century but with some 14th century windows and buttresses, whilst the tower is of c1500, although its west window is probably 14th century work reset. The church has a Norman font with rosettes in medallions and foliage, an old door, a Jacobean pulpit, an old screen now set in the tower arch, some 14th century glass in the south aisle east window and a long iron-bound 13th century chest. The several 18th century monuments include those to Dr Edward Cressett, Bishop of Llandaff, and Sir William Fowler.

CRESSAGE   *Christ Church*   SJ 593040

In the church of 1841 is a pulpit from the destroyed old church of St Samson. It is inscribed "Houmfry Dalle made this for John Dalle; which I pray God bles unto his end. Amen: 1635".

CULMINGTON   *All Saints*   SO 494820

The 12th century nave has herringbone masonry and small windows. It and the 13th century chancel and 14th century tower are all of equal external width. A modern top caps the incomplete stone spire. The recess with ballflower ornament and the roodloft staircase on the south side are 14th century. A Victorian east window replaced a set of tall lancets. The roof has collar-beams in straight braces and double curved wind-braces, and parts of the screen are also medieval. There is a monument with primitive Renaissance details to Ralph Greaves, d1630, and there are many tablets on the chancel walls.

DAWLEY   *Holy Trinity*   SJ 687064

The church of 1845 by Henry Eginton at Dawley Magna contains a Norman font with chevrons, fluted panels and a Tree of Life.

DEUXHILL   *Dedication Unknown*   SO 697872

Behind a farm lies part of the north wall with a 15th century window of a church demolished in the 19th century.

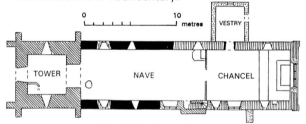

Plan of Culmington Church

Culmington Church   *Culmington Church*

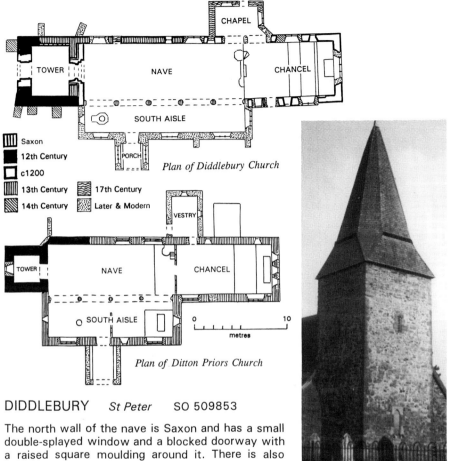

CHAPEL

TOWER   NAVE   CHANCEL

SOUTH AISLE

- Saxon
- 12th Century
- c1200
- 13th Century
- 14th Century
- 17th Century
- Later & Modern

PORCH

Plan of Diddlebury Church

VESTRY

TOWER   NAVE   CHANCEL

SOUTH AISLE   0   10
                    metres

Plan of Ditton Priors Church

Ditton Priors Church

DIDDLEBURY   *St Peter*   SO 509853

The north wall of the nave is Saxon and has a small double-splayed window and a blocked doorway with a raised square moulding around it. There is also Saxon part in the base of the tower, probably part of a west porch. The existing west doorway and tower arch are late 12th century but both are set into older arches. The chancel, which inclines to the north, is 12th century with several original windows still in use or traceable. Three windows and two tomb recess with ballflower ornamentation are early 14th century. The five bay south arcade is 13th century but the aisle itself was rebuilt in 1862, whilst the porch is of 1854. The chancel east window is also Victorian. The vestry is 17th century and the font is 15th century. There are several ancient inscriptions to the Baldwin family.

DITTON PRIORS   *St John the Baptist*   SO 608892

Most of the equally wide nave and chancel and the south aisle and four bay arcade are 13th century, but the west tower and part of the nave north wall are Norman. In its present form the wooden broach spire is of 1831. There are various windows from the late 13th century to the 16th century and the east windows and vestry are of the restoration of 1861. The trussed rafter roof is old and the screen incorporates parts of that from Burwarton. There is an inscription to Thomas Jenks, vicar, d1648.

Edgmond Church

Donnington Church

DONINGTON   St Cuthbert   SJ 809047

The 14th century chancel has some good windows in one of which is original glass including a Virgin and Christ. The nave looks late medieval but may be as late as 1635, the date on the double hammerbeam roof. The north aisle, chancel arch and tower are of the restoration of 1878-80. The tower was originally a late 12th and 15th century building but it collapsed during restoration. In the chancel is a brass plate to Edmund Waring, d1682, M.P. for Bridgnorth and Sheriff of Shropshire. It was reported in 1256 that "Simon, parson of Dunyton" had been slain by unknown malefactors who had also burnt his house.

DUDLESTON   St Peter   SO 566952

A visitation record of 1799 refers to the church as being roughcast and timber-framed. Another record refers to the aisles being rebuilt in 1819, the likely period of the west tower with an octagonal upper stage. Most of the chancel is of 1877, but older masonry survives there and in the slightly projecting east parts of the aisles.

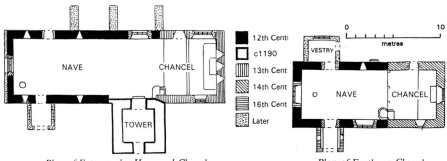

Plan of Eaton-under-Haywood Church

Plan of Easthope Church

EASTHOPE   *St Peter*   SO 566952

The church comprises a 12th century nave with one Norman window and a chancel of the same width of c1300. A simple old screen and a pulpit and pews given by Edward Ball of London in 1623 to his home church were destroyed in a fire in 1923. The hourglass on an arm is a replica of the original dated 1662 destroyed in the fire.

EATON CONSTANTINE   *St Mary*   SJ 597063

Only a Norman font survived the rebuilding of the church in 1841.

EATON-UNDER-HAYWOOD   *St Edith*   SO 500900

The 12th century nave with four Norman windows is undivided from the 13th century chancel with triple east lancets. A north window is of c1300, the south transeptal tower is of c1190, and the oak effigy of a man in civilian costume in a recess with a canopy decorated with ballflowers is early 14th century. In a restoration of 1868 the west wall was thickened at the base, the north wall given three large buttresses and a south porch added. The roofs are old, that over the nave having tie-beams and collar-beams on arched braces, whilst that over the chancel is flatter and lower with bosses. Between the two is a tympanum painted with arms. The pulpit and reading desk are Jacobean, although the former has older parts.

EDGMOND   *St Peter*   SJ 720193

Under a carpet in the spacious 14th century chancel are brasses of Francis Yonge, d1533, depicted in his burial shroud, and his wife and family. The west tower with a quatrefoil frieze between the parapet, four bay arcades, the embattled south aisle and porch with an original door are all 15th century, although the bases and abaci of the north arcade piers are 13th century work reused, and the north aisle outer wall is 14th century. The Early Norman font is decorated with geometrical patterns and loose interlace. The NW vestry and organ loft are Victorian additions.

EDGTON   *St Michael*   SO 387857

The 13th century nave has an original west doorway and window above it. The chancel and vestry are 19th century. See back cover.

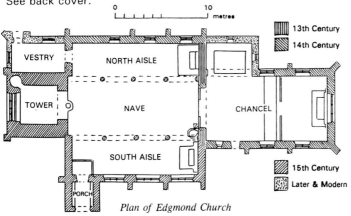

	13th Century
	14th Century
	15th Century
	Later & Modern

Plan of Edgmond Church

Brass at Edgmond

EDSTASTON   *St Mary*   SJ 518320

The nave was shortened at the west end in 1723 and the present west wall was built in 1883. Otherwise both nave and chancel are Late Norman work of some pretension. There are three original doorways, all with nook-shafts, and that on the south side is an elaborate piece with chevron and crenellation ornamentation and a hoodmould on head-stops. In the nave north wall is a window with external nook-shafts and there is a more modest Norman window in the chancel. There are two internal string courses at the level of the sills of the windows and at the springing of their arches. The chancel has a five-light east window and a south window and buttresses of the 14th century. Four other windows and the porch are 15th century. The nave has a fine old roof with tie-beams, kingposts and two tiers of wind-braces. The pulpit is Jacobean, the north and south doors have original ironwork, and there are some fragments of 15th century stained glass in one of the south windows.

ELLESMERE   *St Mary*   SJ 403348

The nave and aisles of this large cruciform church were entirely rebuilt in 1849 by Sir George Gilbert Scott and the remainder was heavily restored in 1881, 1889 and 1900. The oldest part is the Norman east respond of the nave north arcade. The crossing arches and north transept are 13th century and the chancel with its north and south chapels and the south transept, plus the tower top with a frieze below the battlements and eight pinnacles are 15th century. Of the 14th century are the arch from the south transept into the south chapel (in which is a 15th century screen) and the two western arches of the arcade between that chapel and the chancel. The south chapel has a fine old low-pitched roof. The 15th century font has square panels filled with carvings of the Instruments of Christ Passion. There are effigies of a knight of c1300 and of Francis Kynaston of Otley, d1581, and his wife and their children (the latter rather damaged). Above them is a contemporary helm.

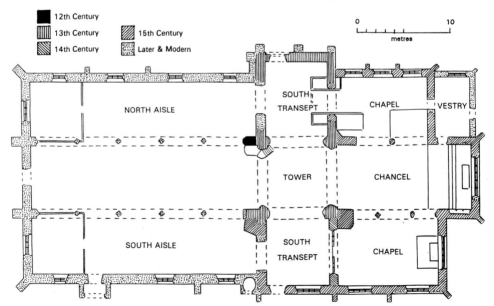

Plan of Ellesmere Church

Edstaston Church

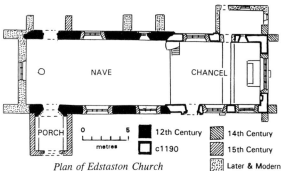

Plan of Edstaston Church

0 ... 5 metres

■ 12th Century
□ c1190
▨ 14th Century
▨ 15th Century
▨ Later & Modern

Ellesmere Church

EYTON-UPON-THE-WEALD-MOORS   *St Catherine*   SJ 651148

The red brick nave, chancel and tower with arched windows and quoins are all of 1743 and inside are contemporary benches, a west gallery, pulpit and panelling. The polygonal apse was added in 1850. In a north window are fragments of 15th and 16th century glass.

FARLOW   *St Giles*   SO 640806

The church of 1858 has a Norman south doorway arch decorated with chevrons.

FITZ   *St Peter & St Paul*   SJ 148178

Built upon Norman foundations are the nave, chancel and west tower of 1722, constructed of brick with stone dressings and quoins. A two bay south aisle was added in 1846 and a piscina of c1200 was reset within it. The chancel was remodelled with round arches in 1905 by Aston Webb.

Doorway at Edstaston

FORD   *St Michael*   SJ 413138

The church lies on a small hill between the Mansion House and Ford House. It is a 13th century building with one lancet window and two original south doorways. The later medieval nave roof has wind-braces arranged to produce cusped circles rather than the usual quatrefoils. There was a drastic restoration in 1875 when the west projection, the small south porch, the north aisle, organ chamber, vestry and most of the windows were added. The screen is 15th century and the reredos is composed of Jacobean parts and carvings by an Antwerp Mannerist of c1530.

FRODESLEY   *St Mark*   SJ 516011

The Norman font is now returned to the church of 1809 with a north aisle of 1859. Inside are early 19th century box-pews and a pulpit.

GLAZELEY   *St Bartholomew*   SO 704883

The church itself is entirely of 1875 by Blomfield but it contains brasses of Thomas Wylde, d1599, and his wife Elizabeth, and there is a Norman font lying outside.

GREAT BOLAS   *Dedication Unknown*   SJ 647214

The stone chancel and the ends of the seats inside it are probably late 17th century whilst the brick nave and west tower, the pulpit and tester, and the west gallery are all of 1726-9.

GREAT HANWOOD   *St Thomas*   SJ 444096

A fluted Norman font lies inside the brick nave and chancel of 1826.

GREAT NESS   *St Andrew*   SJ 397190

The nave south wall has a 13th century doorway set within a short blocked two-bay arcade of the same date. Either an intended chapel was never built or the doorway has been reset after destruction of the chapel. The nave was widened slightly to the north in the 15th century and then given the present roof with collar-beams on arched braces and cusped diagonally-set queen-posts. The porch and south buttresses are probably also 15th century. The 13th century tower has 14th century buttresses and a later top stage. The chancel is mostly of c1300-20 but the reticulated east window must be slightly later. The squint on the north side served a former chapel or vestry.

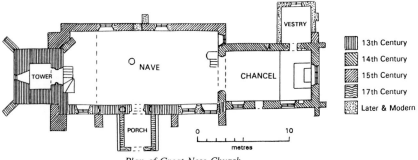

Plan of Great Ness Church

Great Ness Church

Halston Chapel

GREETE   *St James*   SO 577708

The 12th century nave has a much renewed Norman south doorway and 13th and 15th century windows. The chancel is 13th century with three large new south windows inserted in the 1290s. The chancel arch is of the restoration of 1856.

HABBERLEY   *St Mary*   SJ 398036

This small 12th century church was heavily restored in 1864. It has plain Norman north and south doorways and one 16th century window.

HADNALL   *St Mary Magdalene*   SJ 522200

Hadnall was a chapelry of Myddle until 1856. The buttressed 14th century nave incorporating a plain Norman south doorway and a Late Norman north doorway comprised the entire building until the tower was added in the 1830s and a chancel was added in 1873.

HALFORD   *Dedication Unknown*   SO 436834

The church lies above the River Onny. It has a Norman nave with a south doorway with a hoodmould of a chain of crocus-blossom forms. The church was restored in 1848 and was given a new chancel in 1887.

HALSTON   *Dedication Unknown*   SJ 338314

A late medieval timber-framed chapel with a brick west tower added in 1725 lies in the grounds of the hall. The tiebeams inside have short braces with figures in the spandrels, including a bishop, horse, and fox. The west gallery with painted Royal Arms is probably Jacobean with re-used early 16th century parts said to have come from the former rood screen at Whittington. The panelling looks Elizabethan but the box pews and commandment boards are later, and the pulpit is dated 1725, the likely period of the altar rails and the brass chandelier.

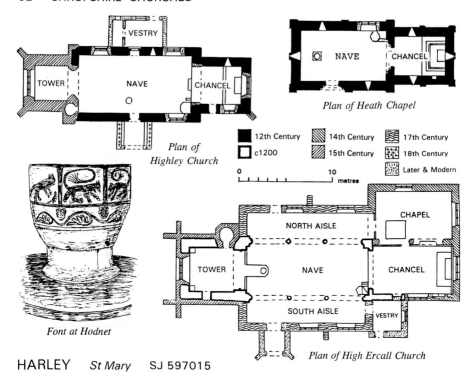

VESTRY

TOWER | NAVE | CHANCEL

Plan of Highley Church

NAVE | CHANCEL

Plan of Heath Chapel

■ 12th Century	▨ 14th Century	▨ 17th Century
□ c1200	▨ 15th Century	▨ 18th Century
		▨ Later & Modern

0   10   metres

Font at Hodnet

CHAPEL

NORTH AISLE

TOWER | NAVE | CHANCEL

SOUTH AISLE | VESTRY

Plan of High Ercall Church

HARLEY   *St Mary*   SJ 597015

The nave and chancel were built in 1846 by S.P.Smith, but the west tower is 15th century and in the chancel is a brass to Sir Richard Lacon, Sheriff of Shropshire in 1477 and 1486, and his wife Alice.

HEATH   *Dedication Unknown*   SO 557856

This small Norman chapel in a field is unaltered except for one 19th century window inserted to give more light to the pulpit. The chancel arch and south doorway each have two orders of shafts and each compartment has three small original windows, the east and west ones piercing two of the many pilaster buttresses. The tie-beam roof is old and one chancel pew contains re-used 15th century parts. On the nave south wall are traces of a wall painting, possibly of St George and the Dragon. Of the 17th century are the pulpit, reader's desk, squire's pew, box pews and altar rails.

HIGH ERCALL   *St Michael*   SJ 595173

The church was severely damaged during the siege of the adjacent hall in 1646 and much of it now dates from 1658-62, with double hammerbeam roofs of that period. Of what until then was a complete Late Norman church of c1190-1200 there survive the three-bay arcades and the tower arch and chancel arch. The 14th century two bay north chapel and most of the chancel were probably paid for by the knight whose cross-legged effigy lies between the two. The south vestry was added during G.E.Street's restoration of 1865. The tower with a quatrefoil frieze below the battlements looks 15th century but it is unlikely to have survived the siege of 1646 intact. A small Early Norman tympanum is reset on the nave north wall.

HIGHLEY *St Mary* SO 436834

The Norman nave and chancel arch each have an original north window and there are two original doorways, one with contemporary ironwork on the door itself. The west tower and east window are 15th century and the porch is 18th century. Four windows and the north vestry are Victorian. Of the churchyard cross there remains a base with cable moulding, heads at the corners and a crocketted niche, plus the shaft.

HINSTOCK *St Oswald* SJ 694264

The church comprises a nave and chancel of 1719-20, a wide south aisle of the 1850s, and a west tower probably of c1800, the period of the pulpit and benches.

HODNET *St Luke* SJ 612287

Much of the church, comprising a wide nave and chancel, an equally wide south aisle, and a very rare octagonal tower, is 14th century. The Norman nave, of which some masonry survives, was what is now the western part of the aisle. There are three parallel gables at the east end, the northern one belonging to the Heber family chapel of 1870. Only the two eastern bays of the arcade are original, the remainder, and most of the windows, being of the restoration of 1846. The font decorated with lions, rosettes, a cock and an eagle looks Norman but is probably actually 17th century. Among the many 18th and 19th century monuments are those to Richard Hill, d1726, at the west end, and Henrietta Vernon, d1752, on the north wall. The south door is dated 1705.

Hodnet Church

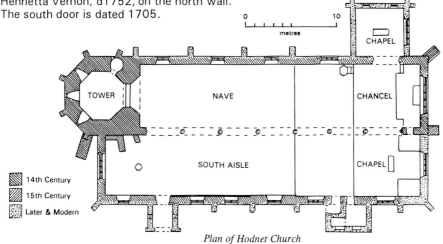

14th Century
15th Century
Later & Modern

Plan of Hodnet Church

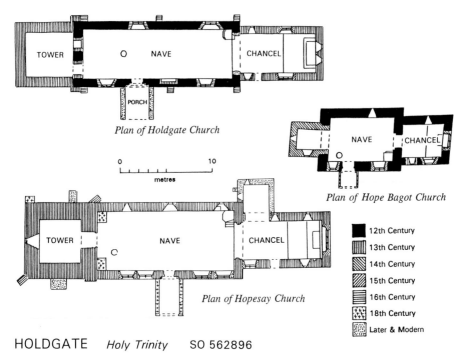

Plan of Holdgate Church

Plan of Hope Bagot Church

Plan of Hopesay Church

■ 12th Century
▥ 13th Century
▨ 14th Century
▨ 15th Century
▤ 16th Century
▦ 18th Century
▦ Later & Modern

HOLDGATE   *Holy Trinity*   SO 562896

The long 12th century nave has a west window now looking into the 13th century tower, a richly decorated south doorway with chevrons, beak-heads and a sort of arched frieze. There is also a 13th century tomb recess and there are several 16th century windows and buttresses. The 13th century chancel has several original windows plus one each from the 14th and 15th centuries, and on the exterior is a sheila-na-gig. The font is a fine Norman piece carved with a dragon, medallion, foliage and interlacing, and there is a Jacobean seat in the nave.

HOPE BAGOT   *St John the Baptist*   SO 589741

This is a delightful little Norman church lying on the southern slopes of the Titterstone Clee Hill. The nave and chancel each have one original 12th century window and are separated by a round arch decorated with saltire crosses, as is the south doorway. There are several 14th century windows and the small west tower may be of that period, and the chancel also has a 13th century lancet and 15th century window. There is a Jacobean pulpit and a small west gallery dated 1726.

HOPESAY   *St Mary*   SO 388833

The broad, low west tower and the chancel with lancet windows are additions of c1200-10 to a nave of c1160 with an original Norman south doorway. The east window and two others are 14th century and three south windows are 19th century. The narrower tower top may be 17th century and the porch is 18th century. The nave has a fine old roof with collar-beams on arched braces resting on a decorated wall-plate, and the chancel stalls are partly Jacobean. A SW window contains the arms of Richard, Earl of Arundel, executed in 1397.

HOPTON CANGFORD   *No Dedication Recorded*   SO 548804

The red-brick tower, nave and polygonal apse are all of 1766. Some contemporary furnishings remain inside, but not necessarily in situ, since the church has been sold off for private occupation.

HORDLEY   *St Mary*   SJ 381508

The nave is 12th century with an original blocked north doorway, and the chancel is 14th century, but the other features are of the restorations of 1850, 1880 and 1885.

HUGHLEY   *St John the Baptist*   SO 565980

The entire north wall of the single body is 13th century, with two lancet windows. The rest is mid to late 14th century and has from that period a fine screen, the roof, and stained glass figures under canopies. In the chancel is a bracket for an image resting on the head of a lady, and also a pillar piscina. The pulpit is Jacobean.

IGHTFIELD   *St John the Baptist*   SJ 593388

Until the chancel was rebuilt in 1865 the entire building was 15th century, a rarity in Shropshire. The original parts comprise an embattled nave, a north aisle with a three bay arcade, a south porch and a diagonally-buttressed west tower with a frieze below the parapet. Inside are a 15th century chest and brasses to William Maynwaring, d1497, and his daughter Dame Margery Calveley, d1495, wife of Philip Egerton. The base of the churchyard cross is unusually ornamental, with quatrefoils and worn corner figures.

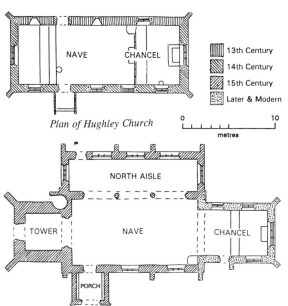

Plan of Hughley Church

▓▓ 13th Century
▨▨ 14th Century
▧▧ 15th Century
▒▒ Later & Modern

0   metres   10

Plan of Ightfield Church

Holdgate Church

JACKFIELD   *St Mary*   SJ 687030

The old church of 1759 by Francis Turner Blyth is of red brick and has a west tower with the parapet raised at the corners and a five-bay nave with windows with Gibbs surrounds and a short chancel with a Venetian east window. The new church of 1863 by Blomfield has red, yellow and blue bricks, and a polygonal bell turret.

KENLEY   *St John the Baptist*   SJ 563008

The single body forming the nave and chancel is Norman and has traces of an original north doorway. The west window and the low pyramidal-roofed west tower are 14th century, and the porch and other windows are early 19th century. The chancel roof is ancient and the pulpit and tester and the reader's desk are Jacobean.

KINLET   *St John the Baptist*   SO 711810

The church lies in trees near the hall, far from the main road. Of the original Norman church there remain two reset window heads in the chancel walls. In the late 12th century a narrow north aisle was added and then in the early 13th century an equally narrow south aisle was added, together with a large south porch and a west tower with clasping corner pilasters. Both the arcades have three round arches on circular piers, the earlier piers being more massive. In the early 14th century a spacious new chancel was added along with north and south transepts. Of the 15th century are the tower top, the much restored timber clerestory of the nave, and one north transept window, whilst the vestry and much of the walling of the aisles is Victorian. The south transept has a fine alabaster figure of the Trinity in a recess in the east window. Nearby is an effigy of c1420, probably of Isobel, daughter of Sir John Cornwall, wife Sir William Lychefield. In the chancel are tomb chests with effigies to Sir Humphrey Blount, d1477, and Sir John Blount, d1531, and their respective wives, and in the north transept is an elaborate canopied tomb with effigies of Sir George Blount, d1581, and his wife Constantia, d1584, plus many tablets to members of the Childe family, notably that of Sir William Childe, d1678.

Kinlet Church

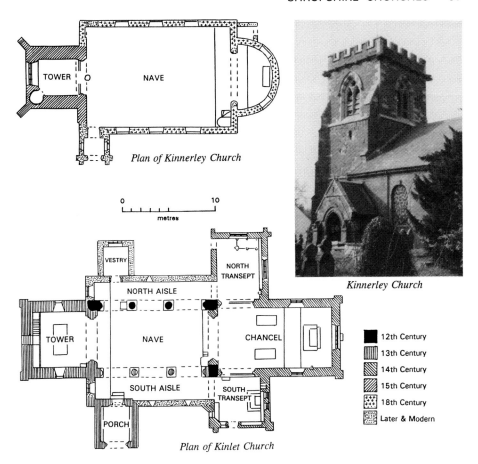

Plan of Kinnerley Church

0 _____ 10
metres

Kinnerley Church

■	12th Century
▥	13th Century
▨	14th Century
▧	15th Century
▦	18th Century
▒	Later & Modern

Plan of Kinlet Church

KINNERLEY   *St Mary*   SJ 339210

The nave and apse designed in 1769 by Thomas Pritchard were built in 1773-4. The west tower is 15th century and the porch, tower upper windows and the chancel arch are of 1887-90.

KNOCKIN   *St Mary*   SJ 334223

The church founded by Ralph Le Strange between 1182 and 1192 has a nave and chancel which were drastically restored in 1847, and given a west porch in 1919, plus a north aisle of which all that remain are the blocked round arches with chamfered hoodmoulds and slender circular piers. The original priest's doorway has a tympanum over a segmentally arched lintel and nook shafts.

Knockin Church

KYNNERSLEY   *St Chad*   SJ 673167

The nave, chancel, and bellcote over the chancel arch are of c1320-30, although the nave windows are mostly 19th century. The west tower is of 1722-3, the latter year appearing on one of the obelisks. See plan on page 60.

LANGLEY   *No Dedication Recorded*   SJ 537001

This chapel was built in 1564 and formerly had a stone bearing that year on the exterior. It still has a roof beam dated 1601. The east window is in the style of those of c1300. The chancel roof is of the trussed rafter type and that in the nave has two tie-beams and three collar-beams on arched braces. The squire's pew, pulpit, benches and pews are all 17th century. The chapel is no longer in regular use and is maintained as an ancient monument by English Heritage. See plan on page 61.

LEEBOTWOOD   *St Mary*   SO 471987

The blocked south doorway declares the main body of the church as 13th century. Two side windows and the narrow oblong west tower are 18th century, and the east window plus one other are Victorian. Within are a number of tablets to the Corbets of Longnor Hall and mural monuments to John Corbet, d1652, and Sir Uvedale Corbet, d1701.

LEE BROCKHURST   *St Peter*   SJ 546272

The 12th century nave has two Norman windows and a south doorway with one order of shafts and chevron ornamentation. Two other windows are 15th century and the chancel, vestry and bellcote are of 1884.

LEIGHTON   *St Mary*   SJ 613051

In 1714 the medieval nave was refaced and re-windowed and given a new chancel. The porch, vestry and belfry are later still. Inside are a late 13th century effigy of a cross-legged knight of the Leighton family, brought here from Buildwas Abbey, a tomb chest with an incised slab to William Leighton, d1520, and his wife Margaret, and a cast-iron slab to William Brown, d1696.

Langley Chapel

Doorway at Lilleshall

Little Ness Church

LILLESHALL   *St Michael*   SJ 728153

The south wall of the long Norman nave has been refaced outside but retains a fine doorway with two orders of shafts and chevrons on the arch. The other Norman doorway east of it is probably reset from the north side where a five bay 16th century arcade now looks into a 14th century aisle. The west tower is 16th century and the chancel is 13th century, although most of the windows and the arch into the chapel at the end of the aisle (now occupied by the organ) are 14th century. The Norman font was restored to use in the late 19th century after a period of exile outside serving as a flowerpot. Built against a former chancel window on the north side is a monument to Sir Richard Leveson, d1661, and his wife Catherine, d1674.

LINLEY   *St Leonard*   SO 687985

The church stands alone amongst trees with only the hall anywhere near. The nave and chancel must represent the church consecrated in 1139 by Robert Bethune, Bishop of Hereford. The west tower with pilaster buttresses rising from a boldly projecting plinth and two-light belfry windows is probably a few years later. The all-Norman effect of the church was slightly spoilt during Blomfield's restoration of 1858 when the south doorway was moved further west (it was originally opposite the blocked north doorway), three large new windows were inserted in the nave, and the chancel east windows were rebuilt. See sketch on page 63.

LITTLE NESS   *Dedication Unknown*   SJ 407198

The church lies within the bailey platform of a small motte and bailey castle. It has a single 12th century chamber with a south doorway with chevrons in the intrados and a blocked Norman north window. Four other windows are 15th century and the west window and vestry are 19th century. Inside are a Norman font, two 18th century chandeliers and an early 16th century German triptych.

LITTLE WENLOCK   *St Lawrence*   SJ 647068

The original nave and chancel are probably 12th century but no Norman features survive. A west tower was added in 1667, a new priest's doorway was inserted in the 18th century, and then in 1865 a new brick nave and chancel were built on the south side, and the tower then given an embattled top stage.

LLANFAIR WATERDINE   *St Mary*   SO 240764

This remote church was a chapel-of-ease to Clun until 1593. It had much carved woodwork until it was entirely rebuilt in 1854. Reset in the altar rail are parts of a screen carved with foliage, grapes, men, women, animals and a Welsh inscription commemorating the donors Sir Matthew Pichgar, Rector of Clun in 1485-20, and his brother Meyrick.

LLANYBLODWELL   *St Michael*   SJ 239229

The church was greatly altered in 1847-50 to designs by the vicar, John Parker. He added an outer skin to the south wall plus a porch and buttresses, the large NW vestry and the almost detached octagonal west tower to produce a building of great character. The new parts almost overwhelm the original Norman main body and the wide 15th century north aisle with a three bay arcade. The font is probably of c1660 and the screen is at least partly 15th century. There are monuments with lengthy inscriptions to Sir John Bridgeman, d1747, and his wife Ursula, d1719, to the widow of Roger Matthews, d1736, aged 92, and Rees Tanat, d1661.

LONGDEN   *St Ruthin*   SJ 442064

The stone nave and brick apse are mostly of the 19th century, but the south doorway and roof are probably 17th century, and the pulpit and font are 18th century.

LONGDON-UPON-TERN   *St Bartholomew*   SJ 623154

The red brick church of 1742 was much altered in the 19th century.

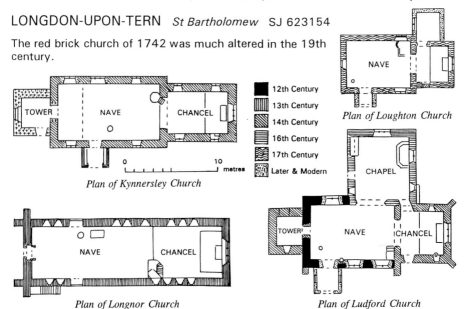

■	12th Century
▥	13th Century
▧	14th Century
▤	16th Century
▨	17th Century
▦	Later & Modern

Plan of Loughton Church

Plan of Kynnersley Church

Plan of Longnor Church

Plan of Ludford Church

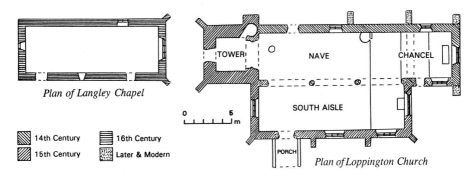

Plan of Langley Chapel

14th Century   16th Century
15th Century   Later & Modern

TOWER   NAVE   CHANCEL

SOUTH AISLE

0   5 m

PORCH

Plan of Loppington Church

LONGFORD   *St Mary*   SJ 726184

South of the disused church of 1802-6 with a west tower, a nave with wide lancets and a polygonal apse, lies the tiny 13th century south chapel of the old church. It has a narrow western arch, a five-light east window and a blocked two-bay arcade which opened towards the chancel. It now forms a Talbot mortuary chapel and contains a large monument to Thomas Talbot, d1686, and his wife, d1706.

LONGNOR   *Dedication Unknown*   SJ 488005

The church is a plain and simple building entirely of c1270-5 except for the 19th century west doorway. The side walls have five groups of lancet windows and two doorways, whilst the east window has three stepped lights with three plain circles above. The box pews inside are dated 1723 and of the same period are the pulpit and reader's desk, and the pews for the families of the squire and vicar.

LOPPINGTON   *St Michael*   SJ 472293

Traces of a Norman building were found during the restoration of 1870. The main body of the church is 14th century with repairs of 1716, and the west tower and south aisle are 15th century. The three bay arcade is of 1870. The south porch dated 1658 replaced a porch burnt during the Civil War when the church was garrisoned by Parliamentary troops and was stormed by a Royalist force. The nave and aisle roofs are also likely to be replacements of the 1650s.

LOUGHTON   *Dedication Unknown*   SO 615831

The tiny nave and chancel are of 1622, that date appearing over one of the windows, but the chancel arch incorporates some 12th century work. The vestry and porch are Victorian and the plain pulpit and reading desk are of the mid 17th century.

LUDFORD   *St Giles*   SO 513741

The church lies close to the bridge below Ludlow and served the adjacent hospital founded after 1216. The west window now looking into the 14th century tower indicates that the nave is Norman but the porch and other features are of 1866, whilst the chancel is of c1300. The large chapel on the north side was added by William Foxe, d1554, and contains a brass showing him and his wife Jane with numerous children. Also in the chapel are monuments to Edward Foxe, erected c1610 before his death, Dorothy Charlton, d1658, and Job Charlton, d1697.

Interior of Ludlow Church

LUDLOW   *St Laurence*   SO 512747

The church lies tucked away in a close with buildings near to its south side and only a narrow opening from the main street, although the 40m high tower is prominent in distant views of the town. The church is the largest and one of the most beautiful in Shropshire with an internal length of 61m and contains many fine monuments and furnishings. At the Reformation there were twenty-one chantry chapels within the church, each served by its own priest.

The church was first established in the early 12th century when the town was founded. By 1199, when further work was authorised, it had a central crossing tower, transepts, a nave with a south aisle, and a short chancel with wide chapels on each side. Some late 12th century masonry remains in the south chapel with a semi-hexagonal string-course and a round-headed piscina. A longer new chancel, still one bay short of its present length, was built in the 13th century, and of the late 13th century is the south aisle outer wall with a doorway and several window embrasures which are now filled with 15th century tracery.

On the evidence of heraldic glass in some of the windows the north aisle is known to have been added at the expense of Theobald de Verdun c1316. The aisle west window has ballflower ornamentation externally which is typical of that period. About the same time was added the hexagonal two storey porch. The only other medieval hexagonal porch in Britain is that of c1330 at St Mary Redcliffe at Bristol. In c1330-50 the south chapel was given a fine Jesse window which still has the original glass, although much restored, and new south and north transepts were built to replace shorter Norman transepts.

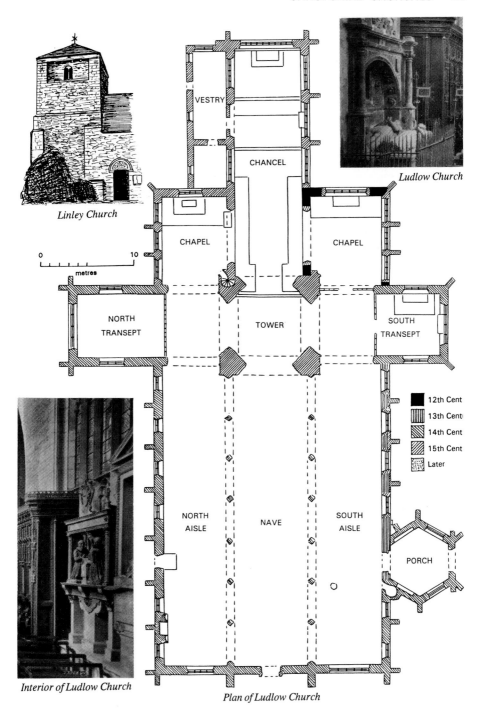

Ludlow Church

Linley Church

0 _____ 10
metres

VESTRY

CHANCEL

CHAPEL

CHAPEL

NORTH TRANSEPT

TOWER

SOUTH TRANSEPT

	12th Cent
	13th Cent
	14th Cent
	15th Cent
	Later

NORTH AISLE

NAVE

SOUTH AISLE

PORCH

Interior of Ludlow Church

Plan of Ludlow Church

The crossing arches, six-bay nave arcades and wide single chapel arches are 15th century work after a fire. The nave was given a clerestory and a new west doorway with a huge window above it, and the transepts heightened and given flying arches to help support the new tower. The north chapel was rebuilt and the south chapel was provided with three large new south windows. The chancel was rebuilt with lofty windows with two transoms, extended by one bay to its present length, and given a series of vestries on the north side. Work on the tower and clerestory progressed until the 1470s but the chancel was probably complete by 1447, when the choir stalls were made. They have miserichords with interesting designs, including a falcon and fetterlock (referring to the then Lord of Ludlow, Richard, Duke of York), a fox in bishop's robes preaching to geese, the Prince of Wales' feathers, a chained antelope (the badge of Henry VI), a mermaid and an ale-wife carried off by a demon. The church was restored in 1839-60 and 1889-91, the work being mostly limited to the removal of galleries and the renewal of decayed stonework, timberwork and glass.

The chancel, chapels, crossing and transepts are all divided from each other by a splendid set of 15th century screens. The south aisle contains a damaged 12th century font and a medieval chest. In the NW corner of the north aisle are two canopied recesses. One is flanked by niches and bears the Tudor rose, giving rise to the suggestion that it may be connected with the burial here in 1505 of the heart of Arthur, the teenage Prince of Wales, eldest son of Henry VII. Filling the north transept is an organ with a Rococo case dated 1764. The north chapel used by the Palmers' Guild has stained glass of c1460 with the story of Edward the Confessor and Palmers. The altar rails here are 18th century, and there is an indent in the floor for former brasses of a merchant and wife of c1500. There is also a tomb chest with effigies of Sir John Bridgeman, d1637, and his wife. In the south transept is a monument with a reclining figure of Mary Eure, d1612. In the 18th century this chapel housed the town fire engines, which were pushed through a now-blocked opening in the south wall. On the screen between this chapel and the chancel are the Ten Commandments, put up in 1561. The chancel has fine bosses on the ceiling and a reredos containing reset 14th century work. There are monuments with effigies of Ambrosia, daughter of Sir Henry Sidney, d1580, Sir Robert Townsend, d1581, and his wife Alice, Edmund Walter, d1592, and his wife Mary, and Edward Waties, d1635, and his wife Martha, and also a monument to Theophilus Salway, d1760.

LYDBURY NORTH   *St Michael*   SO 352860

The long cruciform church has a 12th century nave with two small original windows, two other windows of c1300, an old roof and a late medieval south porch which was rebuilt in 1901. Chevrons in the intrados of the priest's doorway and larger Norman windows date the chancel to c1175. The north transept or Plowden Chapel has a Late Norman arch towards the church but is otherwise all of the early 14th century. The south transept or Walcot Chapel is 17th century, although the windows and the arch towards the church are 19th century. The large west tower is of c1200, but the battlements are later, and there are 17th and 19th century buttresses. Between the nave and chancel is an old screen with a 17th century tympanum above. A second screen of c1500 lies in the north chapel arch, and there is a pulpit dated 1624.

LYDHAM   *Holy Trinity*   SO 352860

The single chamber is 13th century and the trussed rafter roof at the east end is original, whilst the collar-beam roof of the nave is also old. The four south windows and the east window are of 1642 and the porch is Victorian. The pulpit is Jacobean.

MADELEY   *St Michael*   SJ 696041

Parts of a Brooke family monument remain in Thomas Telford's octagonal church of 1796 with a west tower. The nave inside is rectangular, with triangular vestries.

MALINSLEE   *Dedication Unknown*   SJ 698082

Malinslee Hall and the adjacent Norman chapel with original windows in both nave and chancel were removed to make way for the new Telford Town Centre. In 1988 the chapel ruin was re-erected between the two lakes in the Town Park to the south.

MARKET DRAYTON   *St Mary*   SJ 676341

The church comprises a wide nave and chancel with aisles embracing the west tower. The tower once had a stone spire, and, except for the fine nook-shafted Late Norman west doorway, is 14th century, as are the walls of the chancel and north aisle. One pier of the north arcade has a reused 13th century capital with fifteen heads, and the chancel has a reset piscina of c1200-20. The sixteen new windows of 1786 may be the present clerestory. The other features are of 1884.

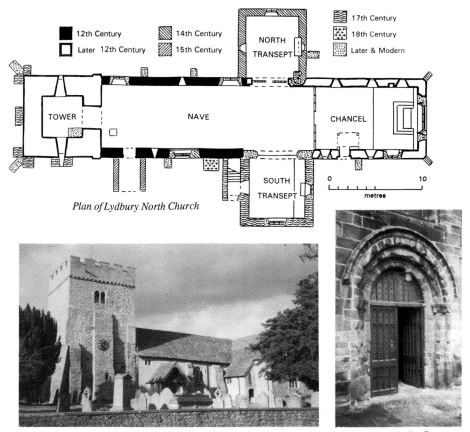

Plan of Lydbury North Church

Lydbury North Church

Doorway at Market Drayton

Milson Church

Melverley Church

MELVERLEY *St Peter* SJ 333166

This is a rare timber-framed church, probably of the late 15th century. It lies by the River Vyrnwy and was much restored in 1878. The church is modest in size but has a barn-like interior divided in half by a simple rood-screen. The west end of the nave is divided off into an entrance lobby and vestry below a west gallery probably of 1588. The windows are all of 1878.

MIDDLETON *Dedication Unknown* SO 540774

The Norman nave and chancel have four original windows but all the other features are of 1851. Inside are a plain Elizabethan pulpit and a rood screen and loft with some old parts.

MILSON *St George* SO 640728

The nave and chancel are essentially Norman with several original windows and a south doorway with scallops and waterleaf on the capitals of the nook-shafts. The low pyramidal-roofed west tower is 13th century, two side windows and the timber-framed south porch are 14th century, and the whole east wall is 19th century. A large lintel high up serves as a chancel arch and the nave has an old tie-beam roof. The pulpit is Elizabethan and there is an old font.

MINSTERLEY *Holy Trinity* SJ 375050

Minsterley was a mere chapel-of-ease to Westbury until 1689 when the Thynnes of Minsterley Hall built a new red-brick church with both Classical and Baroque motifs, rather rustically treated, a great rarity in Shropshire, and indeed the whole of Britain. The church has a single body with battered buttresses, a south porch, and a weatherboarded belfry incongruously perched on top of a fine west facade with a doorway, rectangular windows, and rusticated pilasters supporting a segmental pediment. Contemporary with the church are the doors, altar rail, pulpit and tester, east end panelling, font and west gallery. There is also a remarkable set of seven maiden's garlands dating from 1726 to 1794 made for the funerals of young girls. They each have a wooden frame covered with linen to which are attached white lilies, pink roses, white gloves, and white and blue streamers all of them made of paper.

MONKHOPTON   *St Peter*   SO 626935

The nave and chancel are Norman with several original windows, a 13th century priest's doorway with a trefoiled head and a hoodmould with dogtooth ornament, and one 14th century south window. All the other features, including the porch and the small tower supported on walling inserted at the west end is of 1835 and later. In the church is a brass to Richard Cresset, his wife and family, dated 1640, and signed Fr Grigs. It was formerly at Upton Cressett.

MONTFORD   *St Chad*   SJ 419147

The west tower, nave and chancel are all of 1737-8, designed by William Cooper of Shrewsbury. The window tracery was inserted at the restoration of 1884.

MORE   *St Peter*   SO 343915

The masonry of the west tower and the north wall of the church are 13th century. The More family chapel on the north side was added in the 17th century and the wooden double pyramid top of the tower may also be of that period. The south wall, all the windows, and the north extension of the More Chapel are of 1845 and 1871.

More Church

MORETON CORBET   *St Bartholomew*   SJ 561232

The chancel is Norman but externally refaced in the 18th and 19th centuries, and there is some Norman walling on the north side of the nave. The wide south aisle with a three-bay arcade and a squint towards the high altar, plus the chancel arch, are of c1330-40. A diagonally buttressed west tower was built c1530 but the upper part appears to have been destroyed in the Civil War because it endangered the adjacent castle, and the present top stage is of 1769. Projecting south from the aisle is a chapel containing a squire's pew of c1778. The pulpit and reading desk are both partly Jacobean. In the south aisle are effigies of Sit Robert Corbet, d1513, and his wife, Sir Richard Corbet, d1567, and his wife Margaret, a bust of Richard Corbet, d1691, and a stone to Sir Vincent Corbet, d1680. There is also a monument to Sara, wife of Phineas Fowke, M.D., d1686, from Old St Chad's at Shrewsbury.

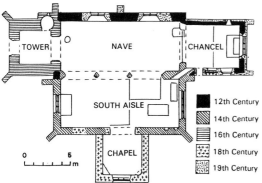

TOWER	NAVE	CHANCEL
	SOUTH AISLE	
	CHAPEL	

0   5
⌐—┴—┴—┴—┴—┐m

■ 12th Century
▨ 14th Century
▤ 16th Century
▦ 18th Century
▒ 19th Century

Plan of Moreton Corbet Church

Moreton Corbet Church

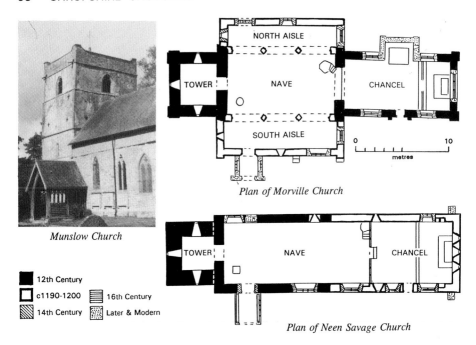

Plan of Morville Church

Munslow Church

■ 12th Century

□ c1190-1200   ▤ 16th Century

▨ 14th Century   ▦ Later & Modern

Plan of Neen Savage Church

MORETON SAY   *St Margaret*   SJ 630345

The round arched west doorway with stiff-leaf capitals on the nook-shafts. now looking into the west tower of 1769, dates the masonry of the church to c1200. In 1788 the stonework was covered outside with a brick skin and given new windows, although the stone east wall is entirely 19th century. The west gallery bears the date 1634, and there is a Norman font. In the NE corner are effigies of Jane Vernon. d1623 and her two husbands, and there is a tablet erected by Jane Grosvenor (nee Vernon) to her two sisters, d1642. There is also a modern monument to Robert, Lord Clive, who was buried here in 1774.

MORVILLE   *St Gregory*   SO 670939

The church is essentially Norman, except for the 19th century clerestory, east window, porch and organ chamber, but of several different building phases. The reset south doorway and the end walls of the nave, including the chancel arch, are likely to be relics of the church built by the monks of Shrewsbury Abbey in place of one mentioned in Domesday Book in 1086. This new church was consecrated by the Bishop of Hereford in 1118. According to Florence of Worcester several of the congregation were killed by lightning whilst returning from the service. The west tower and the long new chancel, both with clasping corner pilasters, are probably of immediately after 1138, when Shrewsbury Abbey established a small dependent cell at Morville. The narrow aisles with arcades of three pointed arches on square piers with four keeled shafts are Late Norman work of the 1190s. The north aisle was given three new windows and a doorway in the 14th century, and the chancel side windows and probably also the tower top are 16th century. The font and south door ironwork are 12th century. There is a 14th century stained glass figure of Christ.

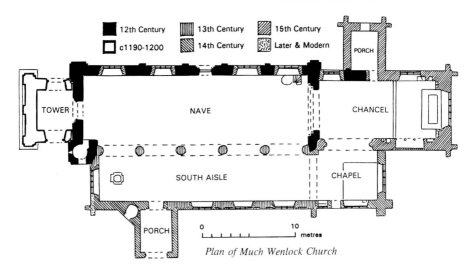

Plan of Much Wenlock Church

MUCH WENLOCK *Holy Trinity* SO 624000

The mid 12th century church comprised the long nave with pilaster buttresses along the north wall, a very ornate west front with a fine roll-moulded, chevroned and nook-shafted doorway, and the western part of the chancel, complete with the restored chancel arch with roll-mouldings and block capitals on the nook-shafts. The staircase at the nave SW corner was intended to serve a tower south of this part of the nave, but in the 1190s a new tower was built in front of the west front. This tower has round arched belfry openings and pointed-arched north and south arches at the base to allow processions around the church without venturing into the street. The spacious south aisle with a five-bay arcade of double chamfered arches on circular piers is 13th century. The two storey south porch and the Lady Chapel east of the aisle are 14th century. In the 15th century the chancel was lengthened and given vaulted sedilia with concave-sided gables, a five-light east window with a crocketted outer gable and side niches for images, a north vestry was added, and the tower given battlements. It was probably in 1744 that the aisle wall was raised and a brick parapet put on the north wall of the nave. The pulpit is Jacobean, the south door has old ironwork, and above the vestry door is a brass plate to Richard Ridley, d1592, and his wife Eleanor and family. See photo on page 8.

MUNSLOW *St Michael* SO 521877

The west tower is mostly Norman with a 15th century topmost stage and an 18th century parapet. The nave south wall is also Norman, but is pierced with a doorway and several windows of the late 13th and early 14th centuries. The chancel is 13th century with one original lancet and two 14th century windows. Also 14th century are the four north aisle windows, although the north arcade is a century later. The font and timber south porch are 15th century, the south door has 13th century ironwork, there is an old chest, some of the bench-ends are medieval, and in a south window are some fragments of 15th and 16th century glass with two seated Virgins and a kneeling family. A slate plate with a shrouded figure between a skull and an hourglass commemorates William Churchman, d1602, and there is a tablet to Richard Baldwin, d1689.

MYNDTOWN   *St John the Baptist*   SO 391896

The roughcasted church lies below the Longmynd. The nave and font are Norman, and the chancel and one south window are 14th century.

MYDDLE   *St Peter*   SJ 467236

Myddle is famous for its historian Richard Gough, who in 1701-6 wrote its story by giving a plan of the church with every pew marked and then giving a genealogical history of those who sat in them. In the chancel is a brass to "arthur Chambre, gentleman, trewe Patron of this Parish Church of Myddle", d1564, and his wife and children, and there is an inscription to Ralph Kynaston, who was rector from 1596 to 1629. The latter offered to pay for part of the cost of rebuilding the tower if the villagers would pay for the rest. They refused, the tower fell down, and the villagers ended up paying the full cost of the tower built by John Dod in 1634. Upon it are many masons' marks. The nave and aisle, divided by a four bay arcade, are of 1744, the year that appears on the nave, but the windows, buttresses, and porch are of 1837-58, whilst the chancel was "renovated" in 1877.

NASH   *St John the Baptist*   SO 604717

The church ranked only as a chapel-of-ease to Burford until 1849. The west tower with a weather-boarded broach-spire has Norman windows, possibly reset, but the main body is 14th century. One old window was reset in the west wall of the aisle added in 1865.

NEEN SAVAGE   *St Mary*   SO 675774

An early 12th century nave with a blocked Norman north doorway and the later 12th century chancel with an original priest's doorway and triple east windows are divided only by a restored early 16th century screen. There are several 14th century windows and one of the 16th century. The 12th century west tower was given a new top stage after the original wooden spire was destroyed by fire in 1825. One window and two buttresses are of 1882. See plan on page 68.

Myndtown Church

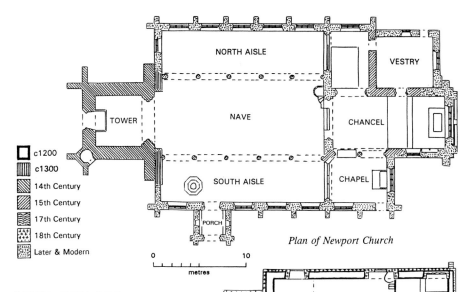

□ c1200
▦ c1300
▨ 14th Century
▧ 15th Century
▩ 17th Century
▦ 18th Century
▨ Later & Modern

0   10
metres

Plan of Newport Church

NEEN SOLLARS *All Saints*

SO 660723

Except for the renewed broach spire with dormer windows at the foot, and the rebuilt chancel of 1859, this cruciform church with trussed rafter roofs, a central tower, and cusped lancet windows is all of c1300. In the south transept is the reclining alabaster effigy of Humphrey Conyngsby, 1567-1610, in armour, a"a perfect scholar by education, and a great traveller by his own affections". See pages 17 & 103.

NEENTON *All Saints* SO 637877

The church itself was rebuilt in 1871 by Sir Arthur Blomfield. It contains a Norman font and a very fine late medieval chest.

NEWPORT *St Nicholas* SJ 745193

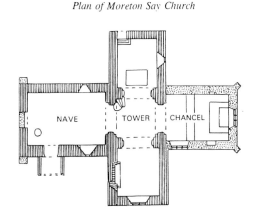

Plan of Moreton Say Church

Plan of Neen Sollars Church

The west tower dates from the 14th century. Much of the rest was built in the mid 15th century, when the church became collegiate, but, except for the responds of the five bay arcades, the two bay south chapel arcade, and some tomb recesses on the north side all was rebuilt again in the 19th century. In the south chapel is a tomb chest with effigies of John Salter, Clerk of the Peace for Salop, d1492, and his wife Isabella, with an inscription nearby. The font is dated 1660.

NORBURY   *All Saints*   SO 364929

The font and west tower are 14th century and under the latter is an old chest. The remainder of the church, including the spire, is of 1880-92.

NORTON-IN-HALES   *St Chad*   SJ 703387

The chancel masonry and the west wall of the south aisle are 13th century, and the diagonally buttressed tower is 15th century. All the rest is of 1864-72. Jacobean woodwork lies in the chancel and reset under the tower is a large monument with effigies of Sir Rowland Cotton of Alkington, and his wife Frances, daughter of Sir Robert Needham of Shavington. She died in childbirth in 1606.

OLDBURY   *St Nicholas*   SO 711920

Most of the church and its furnishings are 19th century but a small amount of thicker medieval masonry survives on either side of the south doorway.

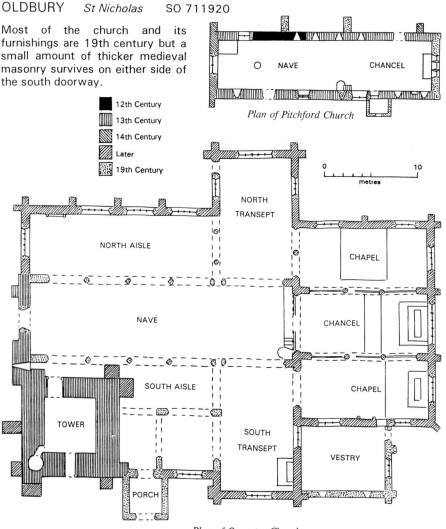

Plan of Pitchford Church

Plan of Oswestry Church

ONIBURY   *St Michael*   SO 456792

The nave and the west half of the chancel, both roughcasted, are Norman, with a plain round arch between them. In the 13th century the chancel was lengthened and given three stepped eastern lancets, and there are other lancets and priest's doorway in the south wall. Also 13th century are the nave north doorway and one window. Two other windows and the west tower are 14th century, and the south doorway and timber porch are 15th century. The nave has an old roof with heavy tie-beams. On either side of the altar are cast-iron slabs with shields and inscriptions dated 1666 and 1673. There is a small mural monument to Dorothy Pitt, d1657.

OSWESTRY   *St Oswald*   SJ 292295

This church almost rivals that of Ludlow in size but is nowhere near as beautiful, being comparatively low and sprawling. The massive 13th century tower in the SW corner was rebuilt at the top with a balustrade and pinnacles in the 1690s. In 1658 the church was exaggeratedly described as "demolisht in the late warrs and layd even with the ground", but a more accurate account of 1685 says the tower was levelled to the height of the main building, the middle of which was destroyed, but the east end left uninjured. The 13th century nave west wall has a lancet squeezed between the tower and the respond of the south arcade. The east window of the 14th century chancel was renewed in 1861. The masonry of the aisles, transepts and chancel chapels is mostly 15th century with late 17th century rebuilding, but the arcades and windows are all of the restoration of 1872-4 by G.E.Street, although the north windows are supposedly reproductions of 17th century ones. The font is dated 1662 and has carvings of a rosette and double eagle. In the north aisle is a monument to Hugh Yale and his wife Dorothy, both d1616.

Oswestry Church

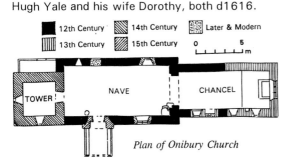

■ 12th Century	▨ 14th Century	▩ Later & Modern
▥ 13th Century	▧ 15th Century	0 ⌐—⌐—⌐—⌐—⌐ 5 m

Plan of Onibury Church

Norton-in-Hales Church

PETTON   *No Dedication Recorded*   SJ 440264

The church was built in 1727 and remodelled in 1870 and 1896. The box pews are of c1727, but the pulpit and tester are Jacobean, and the reredos contains reused 17th century woodwork.

PITCHFORD   *St Michael*   SJ 527043

The church and timber-framed hall are approached down a tree-lined avenue. Part of the north wall with herringbone masonry and one blocked window, is Norman. Otherwise the side walls are 13th century, with three doorways of that period and several lancets. Two side windows and the west wall are 14th century and the classically detailed east wall is of 1719. Inside are a 13th century font, a Jacobean pulpit, reader's desk and benches, a remarkable oak effigy of a cross-legged knight, probably John de Pitchford, d1285, and four incised slabs to members of the Otley family who died in 1529, 1535, 1578, and 1587.

PONTESBURY   *St George*   SJ 400061

Of a large collegiate church of red sandstone with an aisled nave only the large chancel of 1300 survived the collapse of the tower in 1825, a new aisled nave and SW tower being built in 1829. The font, with scallops on the underside, is Norman, and there is 17th century panelling in the chancel. Amongst various monumental tablets is one with a ship to Thomas Davies, a merchant of London, d1674.

POYNTON   *Dedication Unknown*   SJ 570178

Amongst the outbuildings of a farm is the east wall of a chapel with a 15th century window. It lies right alongside a public road.

PREES   *St Chad*   SJ 558335

The chancel, west wall of the nave, and two north windows are of 1864, and the tower is of 1758, but the nave, north aisle and north chapel are all 14th century. The north porch and the windows of the nave and north chapel are 15th and 16th century, one of the latter containing old glass. The tower cuts into the last bay of the arcade of four arches to the aisle, plus two more for the chapel.

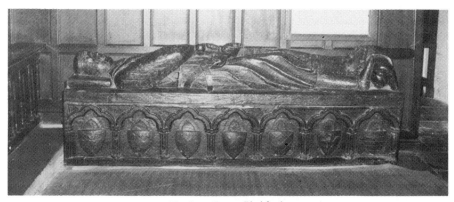

Wooden effigy at Pitchford

PRESTON GUBBALS   *St Martin*   SJ 492197

Only the lowest parts of the west tower, nave and chancel remain, but the 15th century aisle with a blocked four bay arcade of 1866 is preserved, but not in use. It has a reset Norman priest's doorway and an early 14th century stone with a sunk panel containing the bust of a man with an equal-armed foliated cross on his chest.

PRESTON-UPON-THE-WEALD-MOORS   *St Laurence*   SJ 681154

The red-brick west tower and nave and most of the furnishings are of 1739, and the chancel is an addition of 1853.

QUATFORD   *St Mary Magdalene*   SO 739908

The chancel and the fine but worn chancel arch of three orders are relics of the collegiate church built by Roger de Montgomery, Earl of Shrewsbury in the 1070s in fulfilment of a vow made by his wife Adeliza when endangered by a storm when crossing over from Normandy to meet her husband. The windows and buttresses are 14th century. A new nave and embattled west tower were built in 1714 by Henry Pagett and William Higgins, and the south aisle and porch are of 1857.

QUATT   *St Andrew*   SO 756882

The brick west tower, nave, and north aisle are all of 1763, and the three bay north arcade with concave-sided octagonal piers and the chancel windows are late medieval. The chancel masonry may be much older and has a Late Norman priest's doorway, possibly reset. The north chapel was rebuilt in the 1950s but the arch to it may be 14th century. Under the arch is a tomb chest with the effigies of Francis Wolryche, d1614, and his wife, and in the north aisle are a Norman font with cable moulding and the plain tomb chests of Sir Thomas Wolryche, d1668, and Sir Francis Wolryche, d1689, plus the reclining figure of Mary Wolryche, d1678.

Quatt Church

St Martin's Church

RATLINGHOPE   *St Margaret*   SO 403969

It is uncertain how much of this remote church below the Longmynd survived the rebuilding of c1788. The windows all look Victorian, but the south doorway and porch could be of 1625, that date being upon the door itself, and the tie-beam roof could also be 17th century.

ROWTON   *All Hallows*   SJ 616198

The wide church of 1881 incorporates the north and west walls of a much narrower medieval chapel-of-ease to High Ercall.

RUSHBURY   *St Peter*   SO 514919

The nave has a Norman north doorway inserted through Late Saxon herringbone masonry. Of c1200 are the south doorway with waterleaf capitals on the nook-shafts, the west tower and the chancel with original lancets in the side walls and at the east end a set of three lancets separated internally by slim shafts with waterleaf capitals. The various buttresses and nave windows are Victorian. The nave roof has collar beams on arched braces and tie-beams but the chancel has a later hammerbeam roof. The choir stalls are of the 17th century.

RUYTON   *St John The Baptist*   SJ 395223

The 12th century church appears to have once served as the castle chapel. The nave and chancel are both of that period, with two doorways and four original windows in the chancel. In the 14th century the chancel was lengthened by a bay and a north aisle was added with a four bay arcade. Two south windows and the west tower are of c1400, and in the 19th century the aisle was rebuilt and a south porch added. There is a brass inscription to Francis Thornes, d1674, and his wife, d1664.

Ruyton Church

RYTON   *No Dedication Recorded*   SJ 761028

The church lies on a eminence above a stream. The west tower is of 1710, and the chancel is of 1720. Both were restored in 1886, when the nave was rebuilt and a north aisle added.

ST MARTIN'S   *St Martin*   SJ 323364

The sturdy west tower with diagonal buttresses and the north aisle with a five bay arcade are late medieval. The arcade seems to have been built in two campaigns as the eastern arches opening into the chancel are more pointed. The nave south wall is Norman and the chancel is 13th century, with an original priest's doorway. Both are pierced by 15th century windows. The sloping buttresses, porch and NE vestry are of 1810. There are fine 15th century roofs, with boarding in the chancel, and with collar-beams on arched braces with queen-posts forming quatrefoils with the rafters in the nave. Inside there is much pre-mid 19th century woodwork, including a Jacobean three decker pulpit reset at the west end of the aisle.

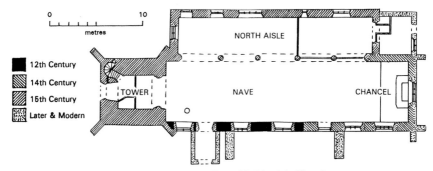

Plan of St Martin's Church

SELATTYN   *St Mary*   SJ 266340

The chancel, with its boarded roof, and the nave windows and roof with collar-beams on arched braces are all 15th century, but the nave masonry is probably 12th century. The west tower was added in 1703 and the north and south transepts were added in 1721 and 1728 respectively. The northern part of the former became a vestry when a new aisle with a five bay arcade was built in 1892. The pulpit and altar rails are 18th century.

SHAWBURY   *St Mary*   SJ 559211

The three bay arcades and the narrow south aisle, and the reset north doorway are Late Norman. The third bay was truncated rather oddly when the west tower was built in the 15th century. It has battlements with a quatrefoil frieze below and eight pinnacles above. Also 15th century is the wider north aisle and north chapel. The large chancel is of the early 13th century and has a blocked priest's doorway, and two blocked lancet windows, a 15th century east window, and other windows of the 19th century. The NW porch is a fine late 17th century piece with rusticated pilasters and two volutes on the gable. There is a geometrically banded Norman font. The pulpit is of 1612, and there is 15th century glass in the chancel.

Shawbury Church

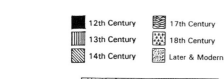

▟ 12th Century	▨ 17th Century
▥ 13th Century	▦ 18th Century
▧ 14th Century	▨ Later & Modern

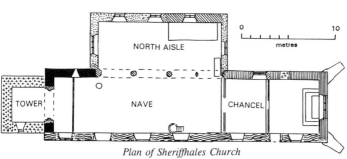

Plan of Sheriffhales Church

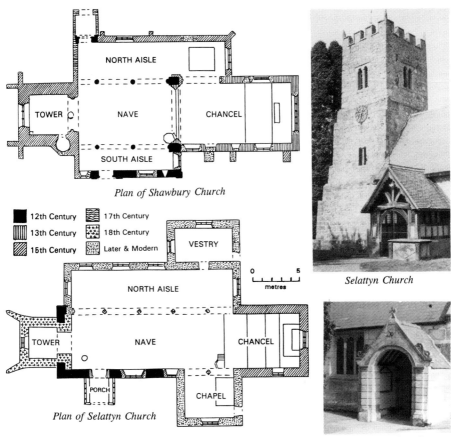

Plan of Shawbury Church

■ 12th Century	▨ 17th Century
▥ 13th Century	▦ 18th Century
▨ 15th Century	▨ Later & Modern

Plan of Selattyn Church

Selattyn Church

Shawbury Church

SHEINTON   *St Peter & St Paul*   SJ 611040

The two bay north aisle, nave windows and most of the chancel are Victorian. Earlier is some of the nave masonry, the wide south doorway, and the chancel north wall, with a 14th century low-side window with a transom. The timber belfry resting inside on posts with arched braces, a tie-beam and quatrefoil strutting, bears the year 1669 with an inscription. The pulpit is Jacobean, and there is a small 13th century female effigy.

SHERIFFHALES   *St Mary*   SJ 758120

The nave has a Norman north window and the chancel east and north walls appear to be of c1300. However, the church was much damaged in the Civil War and materials were brought over from Lilleshall Abbey for the restoration recorded on a nave beam of 1661. The ashlar-faced south wall is new work of that period but the four bay arcade looks like re-used medieval material. Some of the north aisle walling is 14th century, and the rest is 19th century. The west tower of 1721 replaced a tower that collapsed in 1717. In the chancel is a worn memorial stone probably to John Beech, vicar, d1586, and there are fragments of 15th century glass with the arms of the Trussell and Burley families.

SHIFNAL   *St Andrew*   SJ 747075

This church was collegiate in the 12th century and was consequently quite a large cruciform building with a central tower. Of it there remains the south transept with a fine blocked south doorway and a renewed east arch which once opened into an apse, the roof mark of which can still be seen, plus the nave west wall, the chancel arch and the western two bays of the chancel with original windows on the north side which are nook-shafted externally and divided by pilaster buttresses. Aisles with four bay arcades were added to the nave in the mid 13th century. The second arch from the west on the south is lower than the rest and the bay behind is vaulted to support the upper storey of the contemporary vaulted porch which extends over it. The vaults have ribs meeting at stiff-leaf bosses. The west window was inserted later and then c1300 a new embattled central tower was built, smaller than the one probably originally intended for its east arch lies in front of the chancel arch.

In the 14th century the chancel was lengthened with an extra east bay and the Moreton Chapel with an arcade of two bays added on the south. This new work includes sedilia in both chancel and chapel and on the south side of the extra new chancel bay outside is a tomb recess with a crocketted ogival head. At the beginning of the 16th century the south aisle east of the porch was widened and embattled. The north transept was entirely rebuilt after fire devastated much of the town in 1591 and the hammerbeam roofs of the nave and chancel are likely to be of that period. The church was restored in 1876-9 and new NE vestries were built in 1899 probably on the site of a 13th century vestry.

An effigy of Thomas Forster, vicar, d1526, lies in a recess in the chancel north wall, and there is a bust of Magdalen Briggs, d1698. In the Moreton Chapel are tomb chests with effigies of Olive Briggs, d1596, and Humphrey Briggs, d1626, and his wife. The pulpit is partly Jacobean, and there is a chest of 1664.

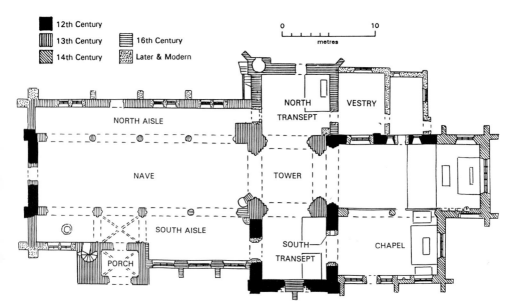

Plan of Shifnal Church

Shifnal Church

SHIPTON *St James* SO 562919

A brass plate records that John, youngest son of Richard Lutwych, in 1589 had the chancel "re-edified and builded of newe from the foundation". So, although it looks like work of c1300-10, this part is Elizabethan and a rare specimen of that period. The nave is 12th century and the plain Norman chancel arch survives, now flanked by small Elizabethan openings. The 13th century tower has a weather boarded upper stage and a pyramidal roof. The nave has a couple of 14th century windows, and a 19th century south porch. The pulpit is Jacobean and there are old altar rails.

SHRAWARDINE *St Mary* SJ 399153

All that survived demolition in 1645 to give the Royalist castle defenders a clearer field of fire was the nave north wall with two 14th century windows and the Norman font. The nave was rebuilt in 1649 but the chancel was not replaced until 1722. Both were given new windows in 1893, when the porch and west vestry were added.

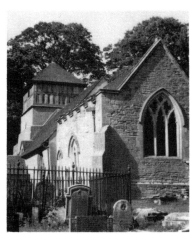

Shipton Church

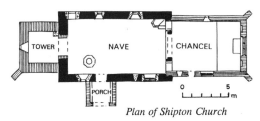

Plan of Shipton Church

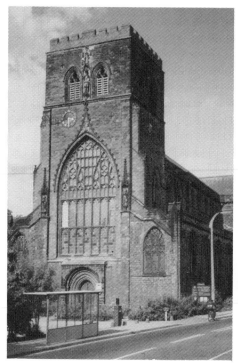

Holy Cross Abbey Church, Shrewsbury

St Alkmund and St Julian, Shrewsbury

SHREWSBURY   *Holy Cross*   SJ 498125

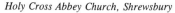

This is the impressive Norman nave of an abbey church founded in the 1080s by Roger de Montgomery. The eastern parts built before his death in 1094 were destroyed at the Dissolution and the present east end is of 1886-7 when the whole building was heavily restored by J.L.Pearson and the only relic of this first phase is the arch from the north aisle into the stump of the north transept with a stilted, roll-moulded arch with scalloped capitals. The nave was built a few years after Earl Roger's death and has vaulted aisles and huge circular piers carrying single-stepped plain round arches with a gallery above and then Pearson's clerestory. The inner part of the early 12th century west doorway has ben altered and the south doorway dates from later in the 12th century. In the late 14th century the gallery arches were filled with windows, new windows were inserted in the aisle walls, and an embattled tower built over the western part of the nave, in the west wall of which a huge seven-light window with a crocketted gable was inserted. In the north aisle are a Norman pillar piscina and remains of the 14th century shrine of St Winifred. There is a three-storey porch on the north side, where repairs were necessary after the Civil War. The font is thought to have been made from a Roman capital. The doors in this porch are dated 1640. Some of the monuments have come from other churches. They include effigies of a priest and lawyer of 1300 and two 13th century knights, plus two late 14th century bearded men in civilian costume, a half-effigy of John Lloyd, d1647, and recumbent effigies of William Charlton, d1544, Richard Onslow, d1571, and William Jones, d1612, all with their respective wives.

SHREWSBURY   *St Alkmund*   SJ 492125

The scare over the collapse of old St Chad's prompted the destruction of the splendid medieval building with the aid of gunpowder, and its replacement by the present church of 1793-5. Designed by Carline and Tilley and Gothic in style, originally with cast-iron window tracery replaced in stone in the 1890s, it has SE and NE porches and incorporates the original 15th century west tower with a noble spire 55m high, now flanked by vestries. Many fine brasses were sold but in 1953 one of c1500 to Margery Humphreston and her two husbands was restored to the church. The oldest of the other monuments is that by James Paget to Sir Thomas Jones, d1692.

SHREWSBURY   *St Chad*   SJ 492124 & 488125

This fine cruciform medieval church on the site of a Saxon building mostly collapsed in 1788 and the only part now standing is the south chapel with east and south walls of c1571, but with arches of c1200 towards the former chancel and south transept. Between these is the massive SE pier of the former central tower. In the fragment of the chancel wall are 15th century sedilia with lierne vaulting. A pit marks the site of the crypt below the north transept, excavated in 1889. Many monuments and fittings were transferred to the surrounding village churches and the only monument of note still here is that to Thomas Edwards, d1634, and his wife.

In 1790-2 a remarkable new round-naved church was erected on a new site further west. Designed by George Steuart, it has rectangular windows and rustication on the lowest level, and round-arched windows at the level of the gallery, which has cast-iron columns. The west tower contains a circular lobby within a square base with Tuscan columns flanked by vestries, a tall octagonal stage above with coupled Ionic pilasters, and a circular top stage with detached Corinthian columns, on top of which are a dome and cross. The oldest and most interesting of the many 19th century tablets is that of John Simpson, d1815, builder of the church.

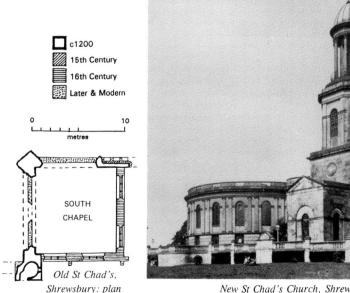

☐ c1200

▨ 15th Century

≣ 16th Century

▦ Later & Modern

0 _____ 10
metres

SOUTH
CHAPEL

*Old St Chad's,
Shrewsbury: plan*

New St Chad's Church, Shrewsbury

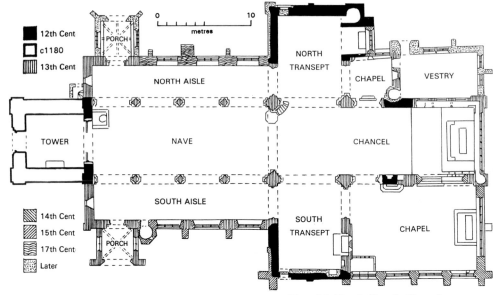

Plan of St Mary's Church, Shrewsbury

SHREWSBURY   *St Giles*   SJ 507118

The 12th century nave and font are relics of the church of a leper hospital situated far outside the town walls on the road to Much Wenlock. The south doorway has thick continuous quadrant-mouldings. The north arcade incorporates two 14th century bays with double-chamfered arches on slim circular piers, and the 15th century chancel arch now lies between the chancel and north chapel. The north aisle, chancel and vestry are of the rebuilding of 1860-4, with additions of 1894.

SHREWSBURY   *St Julian*   SJ 493124

The church itself (now used as a crafts market) was rebuilt in 1749-59 to a Classical design by Thomas Farnolls Pritchard, and remodelled, especially on the south side, in 1846. Of the medieval building there remains only the tower with a red sandstone base of c1200 with arches to the east, north and south and clasping buttresses on the west corners. The yellow limestone upper part is 15th century, and has squinches for an intended spire. In the chancel is a 16th century glass figure from Rouen.

SHREWSBURY   *St Mary*   SJ 494126

Now redundant, but preserved as an ancient monument, St Mary's is the largest and best preserved of Shrewsbury's medieval churches. It lies in a close, prohibiting long range views, but has many beautiful and interesting features. A Saxon church 23m long by 8m wide with an east apse lay on the site. As rebuilt in the 1170s the church had an aisle-less nave, transepts with eastern chapels and a short chancel. Except for the chancel east wall and the south transept chapel the walls of this building still stand, although pierced by later arches and windows, and, in the case of the transepts, partly refaced outside. In the 1180s the large sandstone tower was added. In the 15th century it was given a new top stage surmounted by one of the three highest spires in England. The spire top was rebuilt after collapsing in 1894.

At the beginning of the 13th century aisles were added to the nave and arcades of four round arches on complex piers inserted through the older walls. The aisle west walls each have lancets but the side windows are of the 15th century on the south and of 1658 on the north, whilst the clerestory windows are also 15th century. The vaulted lower storey of the south porch is early 13th century, the upper storey being later medieval. The eastern part of the chancel is early 13th century, although the east window is of 1858. Occupying the whole of the angle between the chancel and south transept is the large mid 14th century Trinity Chapel. The south windows are intermediate between the Decorated and Perpendicular styles. The east window is of 1888. The NE vestry was added in 1884, and the north porch is of 1888.

The church has much old stained glass. The Jesse window in the chancel includes the figures of the donors, Sir John Charlton of Powys and his wife, dating it to c1327-53. It was originally in the Franciscan Friary at Shrewsbury, was transferred to old St Chad's at the Dissolution, and then was moved here in 1792. The glass in the chancel north windows with the life of St Bernard was made for the Cistercian abbey of Altenberg, near Cologne, between 1505 and 1532. Other old glass came from Trier, the Cistercian nunnery of Herchan in the Rhineland, and from St Jacques at Leige. There are also a few fragments of English glass made for the church.

Old fitments include the 15th century font, the doors in the south porch which include parts from the former rood screen, and the organ case of 1727. On the tower west wall outside is a long inscription to one Cadman, d1739, and the monuments inside include a Late Saxon grave-slab with interlace and a cross, an effigy of a 14th century cross-legged knight on a tomb chest, an incised slab to Nicholas Stafford, d1471, and his wife, and tablets to Mary Lyster, d1730, Mary Morhall, d1765, and Richard Lloyd, d1785.

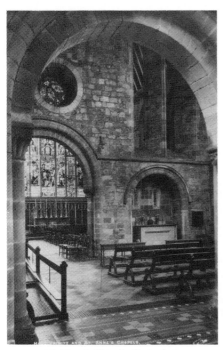

St Mary's Church, Shrewsbury

St Mary's Church, Shrewsbury

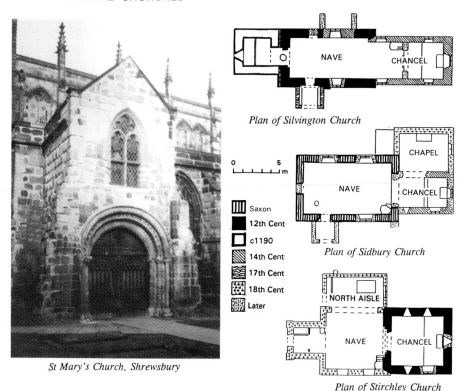

Plan of Silvington Church

0   5
⌐┴┴┴┴┴┐ m

| | | | Saxon

■ 12th Cent

□ c1190

▨ 14th Cent

▧ 17th Cent

▦ 18th Cent

▩ Later

Plan of Sidbury Church

Plan of Stirchley Church

St Mary's Church, Shrewsbury

SIBDON CARWOOD   *St Michael*   SO 413832

An inscription records the rebuilding of the body of the church in 1741. It is approached across the lawn of the castle. The apse and other features are of 1871-2, but the thin west tower is original 18th century work.

SIDBURY   *Holy Trinity*   SO 673829

The nave is Early Norman with patches of herringbone masonry, and the font with intersecting arches and thick, snake-like rolls may be contemporary with it. The chancel masonry is medieval, and the north chapel is early 18th century, with tablets of 1705 and 1708 inside it. The porch and other features are of the restoration of 1878-81 and the second restoration (after a fire) in 1912.

SILVINGTON   *St Nicholas*   SO 621798

The nave has original Norman north and south doorways, the latter with nook-shafts and a thick roll-moulding on the arch. The tower is Late Norman and is asymmetrically set out with its north wall flush with that of the nave and its own east wall built against the nave west wall. The nave windows and chancel are 14th century, but the present (Victorian) chancel arch lies some way east of the position of the original arch, thus increasing the seating space in the church without the expense of enlarging it. The south porch is dated 1662 and the door itself has ironwork dated 1679. There is a tablet to Edward Mytton, d1683.

Doorway at Stanton Lacy

Stanton Lacy Church

SMETHCOTT   *St Michael*   SO 449995

The church has 12th century masonry with a Norman north window and a southern priest's doorway. There is a much later roof with hammerbeams and collar-beams on arched braces, but the porch, buttresses and other windows are of 1850.

STANTON LACY   *St Peter*   SO 496788

The nave and north transept are relics of an early 11th century cruciform church. The transept has traces of one original Saxon window and the nave has a series lesenes or square sectioned strips and a blocked round-headed doorway. A large new chancel was built in the late 13th century and then c1310-20 the tower and south transept were rebuilt. Twenty years year the transept was absorbed into an aisle with a two bay arcade of double-chamfered arches on an octagonal pier towards the nave. The aisle doorway has a continuously moulded arch. Both the aisle and chancel have recesses outside, those in the chancel still containing very worn effigies. There are monuments to Elizabeth Onslowe, d1613, John Thynne, d1717, and Samuel Newborough, d1718.

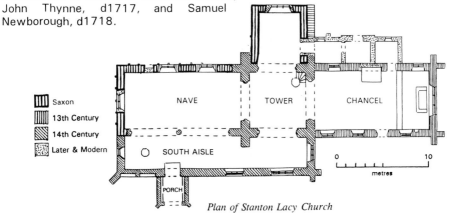

Saxon

13th Century

14th Century

Later & Modern

NAVE   TOWER   CHANCEL

SOUTH AISLE

PORCH

0   10

metres

Plan of Stanton Lacy Church

Stirchley Church

STANTON LONG

St Michael   SO 572907

The nave dates from c1200 and has original south and west windows and a pointed doorway containing a door with original scroll ironwork. The chancel is perhaps slightly later and has both lancets and 14th century windows, and a tomb recess in the south side. The nave roof is ancient, the porch is 15th century, and the vestry and some windows are of 1869-70.

STANTON-UPON-HINE-HEATH   *St Andrew*   SJ 568238

The long Norman nave and chancel have four original windows and two simple doorways. The 13th century west tower has an embattled top stage and pinnacles of the 15th century, plus heavy buttresses dated 1666. The north porch is of 1595, one north window is 15th century, and the blocked two bay arcade remains of a south chapel of c1300. The east wall of the chancel was rebuilt in 1740.

STAPLETON   *St John the Baptist*   SJ 471045

As first constructed c1190-1210 this church was unusual in that it was two storied, having a low and more massively walled lower church and a loftier and more thinly walled upper church above with the floor carried on the internal offset. The building may originally have formed part of the adjacent castle. The priest's doorway of c1300 halfway between the levels suggests that by then the intermediate floor had been removed. There are numerous lancet windows and two original doorways. A west tower was built in 1840 and a vestry and two new windows added in 1867.

Stapleton Church

Stoke St Milborough

STIRCHLEY   *St James*   SJ 699067

The church and its environs form a rustic enclave amidst Telford New Town suburbia. The Norman chancel has original windows (plus one of the 14th century) and a fine chancel arch of three orders adorned with elongated chain links and chevrons. In 1741 the church was given a new brick nave no longer than the chancel, plus a small west tower with clasping corner buttresses and a fresh set of furnishings including box pews, a pulpit and reader's desk. The north aisle was added in 1838.

STOCKTON   *St Chad*   SO 729997

The west tower is 15th century with 17th century upper parts. Externally the church appears to be all of 1860 but some Norman work, including one window, remains in the chancel, together with a 14th century low-side window, and there is a 15th century font.

STOKE ST MILBOROUGH   *St Milburgh*   SO 866823

The church is dedicated to the 7th century founder of Wenlock Abbey. The wide mave and chancel are mostly of the 14th century but the chancel arch and much of the west tower are 13th century, and there are slight traces of 12th century masonry in the nave west wall. Of the 15th century are the embattled tower top, one north window and the south porch. The nave has a barn-like roof with arched braces, collar-beams and queen-posts. One collar is dated 1707.

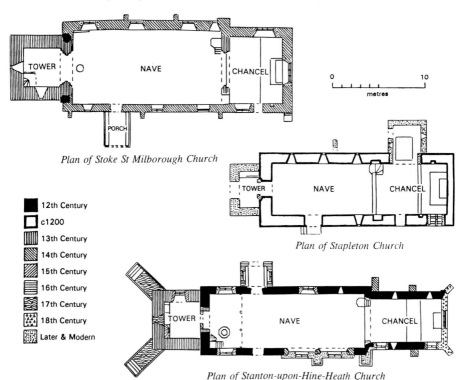

Plan of Stoke St Milborough Church

Plan of Stapleton Church

■ 12th Century
□ c1200
▥ 13th Century
▨ 14th Century
▧ 15th Century
▤ 16th Century
▨ 17th Century
▦ 18th Century
▦ Later & Modern

Plan of Stanton-upon-Hine-Heath Church

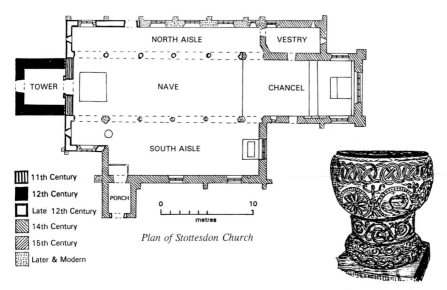

11th Century
12th Century
Late 12th Century
14th Century
15th Century
Later & Modern

NORTH AISLE

VESTRY

TOWER

NAVE

CHANCEL

SOUTH AISLE

PORCH

0   10
metres

Plan of Stottesdon Church

Font at Stottesdon

STOKESAY   *St John the Baptist*   SO 436818

The church is 12th century in origin and the tower arch and chancel windows are late medieval, but substantial rebuilding was needed after damage sustained during the Civil War. Two nave south windows are of 1654, the tower was rebuilt in 1664, and the same date appears on the chancel roof. Also of that period are the nave ceiling, and most of the furnishings, including the pulpit, a canopied squire's pew and the boards with the Commandments, Creed and Exodus Chapter XX.

STOKE-UPON-TERN   *St Peter*   SJ 638280

The large church is entirely of 1874-5. It contains a large tomb chest with recumbent alabaster effigies of Sir Reginald Corbet, Justice of the King's Bench, d1566, and his wife Alice.

STOTTESDON   *St Mary*   SO 673828

This is an interesting church, and the largest in its district. Of an 11th century building there remains the west wall and doorway with a tympanum with saltire crosses and two beasts in profile. By the early 12th century a west tower had been built against it. This has a late medieval top state and battlements. In the late 12th century the nave was given north and south aisles with arcades of five round arches on circular piers with square abaci. Of this there remains the north arcade and the western part of each aisle with small west windows. The south arcade and most of the north wall date from the restoration of 1868. A large new chancel with a north vestry was built c1300-30, and then the four eastern bays of the south aisle were rebuilt almost double their previous width and a south porch added on. The font of c1160 is the finest in Shropshire, with interlacing, bands of scrolls and leaves, and a series of medallions with the Lamb and Cross, beasts, leaf motifs and a frontal figure of a man. There are fragments of 14th century glass in the south aisle, and the pulpit is Jacobean.

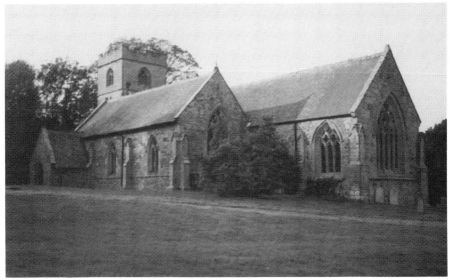

Stottesdon Church

STOWE *St Michael* SO 311737

The thick nave walling may be Norman. The roofs are partly old and there is a date stone of 1581, but everything else is 19th century.

SUTTON *St John* SJ 503103

The 13th century chancel, now closed with a brick west wall, lies in the garden of a house south of Shrewsbury. The Elizabethan roof has one tie-beam connected with the collar-beam by three posts. Inside are a plain Norman font and a communion rail of 1582.

SUTTON MADDOCK

St Mary SJ 719015

The church is all of 1888, except the embattled tower which is dated 1579.

TASLEY

St Peter & St Paul SO 697942

The yellow-brick church was built in 1840 by Josiah Griffith. In it are a 15th century screen and a Jacobean pulpit.

Sutton Maddock Church

Tomb at Tong Church

Brass at Tong

TONG   *St Bartholomew*   SJ 795074

Except for the 13th century south arcade and the Vernon Chapel of c1515 on the south side, the whole church dates from 1410, when Elizabeth, widow of Sir Fulke Pembrugge of Tong Castle founded a college here in his memory. The church has a nave with three bay aisles, a south porch, a central tower flanked by an extra bay of the aisles rather than proper transepts, and a chancel with a north vestry. The church is all-embattled with pinnacles. The tower turns octagonal above the crossing arches and is finished with battlements around the base of a short spire. On the north side is a blocked doorway and evidence of the church having been hit by a cannon ball and several musket shots during a Civil War skirmish. The ruined wall to the west is all that remains of the college buildings, which lay mostly on the south side.

Contemporary with the church are the font with shields, various screens, the vestry door, and the chancel stalls with miserichords mostly carved with foliage but some having angels, an eagle, and the Annunciation. There is a pulpit of 1629.

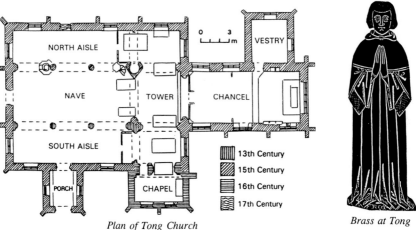

Plan of Tong Church

Brass at Tong

Tomb at Tong Church

The middle of the church is almost filled with monuments. There are incised slabs to a 13th century priest and to Humphrey Vernon, d1542, and his wife. There are brasses to the priests Ralph Elock, d1510, and Arthur Vernon, d1517, and also of Sir William Vernon, d1467, and his wife Margaret set on a tomb chest. There is also a bust of Arthur in a niche in the chapel, quite a rarity for the early 16th century. There are effigies of the founders Sir Fulke and Lady Elizabeth de Pembrugge, and of Sir Richard Vernon of Haddon Hall, d1451, and his wife, Sir Harry Vernon, d1515, for whom the superb fan-vaulted chapel was built, and a two-tier monument to Sir Edward Stanley, d1632, and his parents Margaret Vernon and Sir Thomas Stanley, d1576, plus a relief portrait of Elizabeth Pierrepont, d1696, and the kneeling figure of Mrs Wylde, d1624. There is also a monument to George Vernon, d1780.

Tong Church

Tomb recesses at Tugford

TUGFORD   *St Catherine*   SO 557870

The Norman nave with the north doorway and small window is likely to represent the church mentioned in 1138. The south doorway, flanked by a pair of heads outside, is late 12th century. A lancet dates the chancel to c1200, although the side windows and recesses for effigies are all late 13th century and the east wall is 14th century. The west tower and font are also 13th century. The bier is dated 1617 and part of the screen is reset in the west gallery.

UFFINGTON   *Holy Trinity*   SJ 528138

The church is entirely of 1856 by S.P.Smith but the windows contain 16th and 17th century glass from the Netherlands and Germany.

Tugford Church

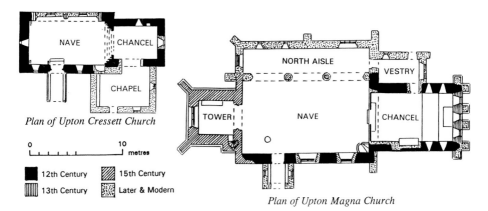

Plan of Upton Cressett Church

0 _____ 10 metres

■ 12th Century   ▨ 15th Century
▨ 13th Century   ▨ Later & Modern

Plan of Upton Magna Church

UPPINGTON   *Holy Trinity*   SJ 597094

The nave has an Early Norman north doorway and the chancel has a Norman south window. Two south windows and the reset west window in the tower are 16th century, and the porch is of 1678. The porch may have been moved during the 1885 restoration when the nave seems to have been lengthened and the tower added on. The east wall and the vestry are also of that date. The arms of Francis, Earl of Bradford, 1680, appear in one of the north windows.

UPTON CRESSETT   *St Michael*   SO 656925

This isolated church, alone except for the hall, is now maintained by the Redundant Churches Fund. During the period when the church lay derelict the brass in the 13th century south chapel was removed to Monkhopton. There is a wall painting on the chapel west wall and a priest's doorway faces south. The Norman nave and chancel are divided by a chancel arch of three orders with chevrons, and there is a similar south doorway flanked with renewed windows with nook-shafts. On the north side are two blocked arches of a former 13th century aisle. The chancel east window is also 13th century. The timber south porch is also ancient. See inside front cover.

UPTON MAGNA   *St Lucy*   SJ 553125

The dedication is a rare one. The chancel has two small Norman windows on each side and the nave has a Norman south wall with a doorway. The east wall with three lancets is 13th century, two south windows are 14th century, and the ashlar-faced and embattled tower with a quatrefoil frieze near the top is 15th century. The north aisle, vestry, east buttresses and south porch are of 1856. There is a monument to Thomas Barker, d1644.

WELLINGTON   *All Saints*   SJ 651117

The medieval church with a pyramidal-roofed west tower and a 14th century east window flanked by 15th century windows in the chapels was demolished in 1789. In the following year work began on a Classical style building design by George Steuart. It has a tower over a west front with a pediment and huge Tuscan pilasters. The sides have five bays of windows in two tiers united into blank arches, and there is a shallow east apse. The altered interior has galleries on cast-iron columns.

WEM   *St Peter & St Paul*   SJ 512288

The 14th century west tower has a west window of a debased Gothic type dated 1667, and late medieval battlements and pinnacles. The new nave of 1809-13 corresponds in width to the medieval nave and south aisle and contains galleries on iron columns. The apsidal chancel and flanking vestries are of 1886.

WENTNOR   *St Michael*   SO 384927

The nave west and north walls with a blocked doorway and a small window are Early Norman, the south doorway is of c1200, and of the 15th century is the roof with tie-beams and collar-beams on arched braces. There is a Jacobean pulpit.

WESTBURY   *St Mary*   SJ 355094

Part of the nave south wall is Norman. In the 13th century it was lengthened and given a new chancel and an aisle with a five bay arcade. The aisle was widened in the 15th century and a new tower built in 1753. It has a Venetian west window above a doorway with a rusticated surround. The heavy buttresses around the church are also probably 18th century. In 1878 the north porch and the vestry were added and most of the windows renewed. There are numerous minor monuments to members of the Corbet, Topp and Severne families.

Wem Church

Westbury Church

WESTON   *St Luke*   SJ 565288

The church dates from 1791 but only the tower betrays that date, since the nave windows are later and the chancel is an addition of 1879.

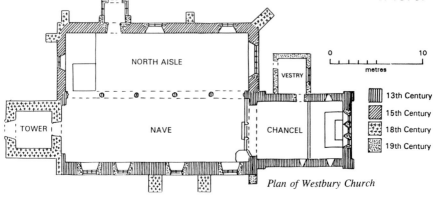

NORTH AISLE

VESTRY

0   10

metres

TOWER   NAVE   CHANCEL

|||| 13th Century

/// 15th Century

18th Century

19th Century

Plan of Westbury Church

West Felton Church

Chancel arch at Wheathill

WEST FELTON *St Michael* SJ 342252

Inside the church are four bay Norman arcades. That on the north side is of c1140 with study round piers with square capitals and abaci, whilst that on the south of c1180-90 has smaller piers with octagonal capitals. The 15th century roof has collar beams on arched braces with queen-posts making lozenge patterns with the rafters. In 1782 the tower collapsed, crushing one of the north arches, and was replaced by a new tower with arched and circular windows. In 1798 it was determined that "the isles be taken down and a stone wall be built between the pillars with decent windows". A new north aisle and chancel were built in 1841 and a narrow south aisle with a porch was erected in 1879.

WHEATHILL *Holy Trinity* SO 622822

The Norman nave and chancel have a narrow roll-moulded arch between them and a similar south doorway. The chancel has one original window, plus two others and a priest's doorway of the 14th century. The nave has a fine 17th century roof with tie-beams and queen-posts connected by round arches. The other windows, the west buttresses and the porch date from the 19th century restoration.

WHITCHURCH *St Alkmund* SJ 542417

The medieval church collapsed in 1711 and was replaced in 1712-3 by a new church designed by John Barker. It is a large building with a semicircular porch attached to its south side. The latter was rebuilt in 1925, but to the old design. The organ case is also early 18th century but the font with a Tudor rose and the Prince of Wales' features is 17th century. Amongst the monuments are effigies of John Talbot, first Earl of Shrewsbury (of a new creation), killed at Chantillon, near Bordeaux in 1453, and Sir John Talbot, rector, founder of the local grammar school, d1550. There are also tablets to Christopher Talbot, Archdeacon of Chester, Matthew Fowler, d1677, and Philip Henry, d1696. See photos on pages 9 and 10.

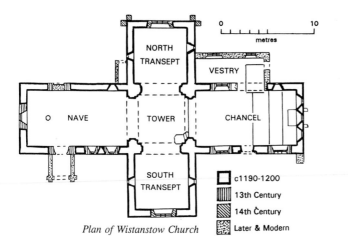

Plan of Wistanstow Church

Brass at Withington

WHITTINGTON   *St John the Baptist*   SJ 326313

The west tower is of 1747, the nave is of 1804, and there are many features of 1894, but nothing remains of the medieval building and its contents.

WHITTON   *St Mary*   SO 576728

The Norman nave has a plain south doorway and three original small windows. Two windows and the short west tower are 14th century and there is an old roof. The chancel east bay and vestry are of 1891.

WILLEY   *St John*   SO 672992

The church is tucked away behind the estate buildings of the hall. The long narrow nave and chancel are 12th century. Both have Early Norman windows, that near the nave west end proving that the nave is of one build and not extended later. Opposite it is a 16th century window. The embattled tower is 18th century. The church takes most of its character from the aisles and family chapel built in 1880 by Sir Arthur Blomfield. There is Jacobean woodwork inside and a monument to one of the Welds

WISTANSTOW   *Holy Trinity*   SO 433856

Most of this cruciform church dates from c1190-1210. Some of the lancet windows are pointed but those in the south transept, which has an original trussed-rafter roof, are round-headed. The priest's doorway with nook-shafts with capitals of upright leaves and a beast's head and a hoodmould with dogtooth ending in two heads is probably reset from the nave. Some windows are late 13th century and of the 14th century are the north transept end wall, the tower arches and the south transept end window. The roofs of the nave and chancel are of 1630. The tower top is of 1712.

WITHINGTON   *St John the Baptist*   SJ 577130

Fixed upon the walls of G.E.Street's church of 1874 are brasses to John Onley, d1512, and his wife Joan, and Adam Grafton, Master of Battlefield College, "the most worshipful prest lyvying in his days" (but also a noted pluralist), d1530.

WOODCOTE   *Dedication Unknown*   SJ 767145

Beside Woodcote Hall is a 12th century chapel with a blocked west window and a fine south doorway with two orders of shafts with shaft-rings. The building was refaced externally and given new windows and buttresses during the 16th and 17th centuries. The windows in the east and west walls and the vestry are 19th century. There are various memorials to the Cotes family, the most notable being the incised slab to Humphrey Cotes, killed at Bosworth in 1485 fighting for the future Henry VII, and his wife Ellen, d1500.

WOOLSTASTON   *St Michael*   SO 453985

The narrow nave and chancel are 13th century with several lancet windows and two south doorways. Two 12th century fonts are set one inside the other. The vestry and four other windows are Victorian.

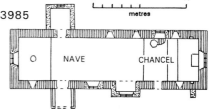

Plan of Woolstaston Church

WORFIELD   *St Peter*   SO 758958

This is a very large church for a small village. Some 13th century masonry remains at the west end of a former long unaisled nave and there is a Norman fragment near the chancel arch, but the rest is of several phases during the 14th century, the chancel and transepts being built first. The transepts were later absorbed into wide aisles with a five bay north arcade and a four bay south arcade. Finally a large tower and lofty spire were built in the SW corner, there being insufficient space beyond the west wall. The south aisle was refaced in 1861-2, when a new porch and organ recess were added. There are fragments of 14th century glass, a 15th century font, a partly original screen, and in the NW corner are tombs with alabaster effigies of George Bromley, d1588, and Sir Edward Bromley, d1626, and their wives.

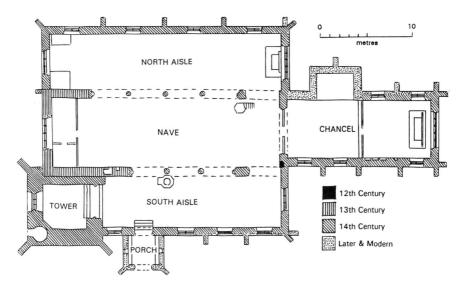

Plan of Worfield Church

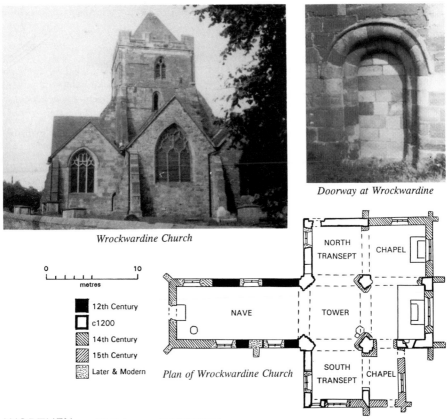

Doorway at Wrockwardine

Wrockwardine Church

Plan of Wrockwardine Church

12th Century
c1200
14th Century
15th Century
Later & Modern

WORTHEN   *All Saints*   SJ 355094

The church has an unusual layout. The 13th century nave is very wide and has an original south doorway, although all the windows and buttresses are of the 19th century. In the middle of the north side is a late 12th century tower with a 15th century top and an 18th century parapet. William Bromshill left money towards work on the tower in 1429. The brick chancel is of 1761 and the south porch with balustraded sides is 17th century. Inside are Jacobean pews and benches and a monument to Dr Daniel Price, Dean of Hereford, Chaplain to Charles I, d1633.

WROCKWARDINE   *St Peter*   SJ 625121

The nave has 12th century masonry, an early 14th century west end, and Victorian windows and buttresses. The church was made cruciform in the 1190s by adding a crossing tower, transepts and a short new chancel. Arches in the transept west walls suggest the intention to added aisles to the nave. There are original doorways in the end walls of the transepts and one lancets remains in the chancel south wall. The east window and buttresses and the embattled tower top are early 14th century, and the north chapel is late 14th century. Of the 15th century are the south transept end wall with a three-light window and the south chapel. The pulpit is Jacobean. There is a Rococo style tablet to William Chudde, d1765.

Tomb at Wroxeter

WROXETER   *St Andrew*   SJ 564083

Part of the north wall of the nave is Saxon work with reused Roman stones. In c1170-80 a fine new chancel, longer and wider than the Saxon nave was added. Four of its original six side windows, and the priest's doorway with nook-shafts and chevrons on the arch, still remain. The Saxon nave was lengthened in the 13th century and there are three north windows of that period, plus one of the 15th century, whilst the chancel has windows of the 14th and 16th centuries. Also 16th century is the diagonally-buttresses and embattled west tower with a NE stair-turret. A south aisle was added at some time but was abolished in 1763 when the present south wall was built further out to create a wider nave. The windows on this side, and the vestry and porch are Victorian. The large font probably originally formed the base of a Roman column. The pulpit and box pews are Jacobean, the altar rail is of 1637, and the iron-bound chest is 13th century. There is also part of a Saxon cross.

In the chancel are four major monuments, three with effigies of Lord Justice Bromley, d1555, and his wife, Sir Richard Newport, d1570, and his wife Margaret, d1598, and John Barber and his wife, d1618, and the other with mourning putti to Francis Newport, Earl of Bradford, d1708. There are several other 17th and 18th century memorials to members of the Newport family.

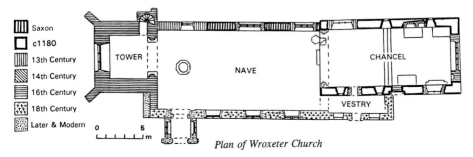

Plan of Wroxeter Church

OTHER ANGLICAN CHURCHES IN SHROPSHIRE

ALL STRETTON - St Michael - 1902 by A.E.Lloyd Oswell.
ASH - Christchurch - Tower & nave 1836 by George Jenkins. Chancel added 1901.
BATCHCOTT - 1891-2 Rockfaced. Good example of design by R. Norman Shaw.
BAYSTONHILL - Christchurch - 1843 by Edward Haycock. Chancel added in 1886.
BETTON STRANGE - 1858. Lancets. Close to Betton Hall.
BROSELEY - All Saints - 1845 by H.Eginton. Large, late medieval style.
CALVERHALL - Holy Trinity - Dated 1872 & 1878. By Eden Nesfield.
CHAPEL LAWN - St Mary - 1844. Lancet-style building by Edward Haycock.
CHETWYND - St Michael - 1865-7 by Benjamin Ferrey. Big, rockfaced. Broach-spire.
CHURCH ASTON - St Andrew - 1867 by G.E.Street. Nave and north aisle.
CLEETON ST MARY - St Mary - 1878 by T.Nicholson.
CRUCKTON - 1840 by Haycock. Nave & chancel with lancets. West porch.
CWM HEAD - St Michael - 1845 by H.C.Whitling. Neo-Norman. Apse & NE tower.
CYNYNION - Christ Church - 1838, but mostly of 1886 except for the tower.
DAWLEY PARVA - St Luke - 1845 by R.Griffiths. Brick nave with apse.
DODDINGTON - St John - 1849. Similar to Hopton Wafers nearby.
DONNINGTON WOOD - St Matthew - 1843 by Sir G.G.Scott. Cruciform with lancets.
DORRINGTON - St Edward - 1845 by E.Haycock. Tower with recessed spire.
DUDLESTON HEATH - St Matthew - 1874 by W.G.MacCarthy.
FAULS - Immanuel - 1856 by Benjamin Ferrey. Nave, chancel, north transept.
FRANKTON - St Andrew - 1858 by E. Haycock. Nave, chancel, SW tower with spire.
GODOWEN - All Saints - 1928, nave extended 1934, tower added 1945.
GRINSHILL - All Saints - 1839-40 by J.Carline Junior. Neo-Norman. Thin tower.
HADLEY - Holy Trinity - 1856 by Owen. Red & yellow brick with lancets.
HENGOED - St Barnabas - 1849-53 by Rev Albany Rossendale Lloyd.
HOPE - Holy Trinity - 1843 by Edward Haycock. Single chamber with lancets.
HOPE BOWDLER - St Andrew - 1863 by S.Pountney Smith. Kempe glass 1888-96.
HOPTON CASTLE - St Mary - 1871 by Charles Nicholson.
HOPTON WAFERS - St Michael - 1827. Tower, nave, chancel. Remodelled later.
IRONBRIDGE - Holy Trinity - 1850-4 by Reeves & Voysey. Fine location.
KEMERTON - St John Baptist - 1882 by J. Farmer. West tower added 1908.
KETLEY - St Mary - 1838. Cruciform with a west tower with low pyramidal roof.
KNOWBURY - St Paul - 1839, altered 1885. Font may be older.
LAWLEY - St John - 1865 by John Ladds. Apse. Red & Yellow brick.
LEATON - Holy Trinity - 1859 by S. Pountney Smith. NW tower and north aisle 1872.
LITTLE STRETTON - All Saints - 1903. Timber framed.
LLANYMYNECH - St Agatha - 1845 by Penson. Neo-Norman. NW porch-tower.
LUDLOW - St John - 1881 by Blomfield. At Gravel Hill.
LYNEAL - St John Evangelist - 1870 by Street. Delightfully placed by a lake.
MAINSTONE - The masonry is Victorian but the roof and chest are medieval.
MALINSLEE - St Leonard - 1805. Elongated octagon with west tower.
MEOLE BRACE - Holy Trinity - 1867-8 by E.Haycock Junior. Large, rockfaced.
MIDDLETON-IN-CHIRBURY - Holy Trinity - 1843 by E. Haycock. Cruciform, apse.
MIDDLETON SCRIVEN - St John Baptist - 1843-8 Nave & chancel.
NEWCASTLE - St John Evangelist - 1848 by Edward Haycock. Lancets.
NEWTOWN - King Charles Church - 1869 by Edward Haycock Junior.
OAKENGATES - Holy Trinity - 1855 by Harrison.
OAKENGATES - St George - 1861. A fine early work of G.E.Street.
OSWESTRY - Holy Trinity - 1836-7 by R.K.Penson. Altered 1894 (tower, etc)
PEPLOW - Chapel of the Ephiphany - 1879 by Norman Shaw.
PRIOR'S LEE - St Peter - 1836 by Robert Ebbles. Lancets, brick, thin tower.
RODINGTON - St George - 1851. Polygonal apse. Corbelled-out belfry.

SAMBROOK - St Luke - 1856 by Benjamin Ferrey. Nave, chancel, north aisle.
SHELTON - Christ Church 1854 by Edward Haycock.
SHELVE - All Saints - 1839. Tower, nave and chancel.
SHREWSBURY - All Saints - 1875-6 by Edward Haycock Junior. Big aisled nave.
SHREWSBURY - St - George - 1832 by E.Haycock. In Drinkwater St, Frankwell.
SHREWSBURY - St Michael - 1829 by John Carline. Yellow brick. at Spring Gardens
SHREWSBURY - Holy Trinity - 1885 by A.E.Lloyd Oswell. In Bellevue Road.
TIBBERTON - All Saints - 1842 by J.Baddeley. Tower, nave and chancel. Red ashlar.
TILSTOCK - Christ Church - 1835. Red brick. Thin west tower with tall pyramid roof.
TREFONEN - 1821-8. Remodelled and chancel and apse added in 1876.
TUCK HILL - Holy Innocents - 1865 by St Aubyn. Nave, chancel, timber bellcote.
WATERS UPTON - St Michael - A minor effort by G.E.Street.
WELLINGTON - Christ Church - 1838 by Thomas Smith. Similar to Ironbridge church.
WELSHAMPTON - St Michael - 1863 by Sir George Gilbert Scott. Good glass in apse.
WESTON LULLINGFIELD - Holy Trinity - 1857 by Edward Haycock Junior.
WESTON RHYN - St John the Devine - 1878 by H.Kennedy.
WHITCHURCH - St Catherine - 1836. Grecian style. At Dodington.
WHIXALL - St Mary - 1867 by G.E.Street. Red brick also exposed inside.
WOORE - St Leonard - 1830 by G.E.Hamilton. Chancel rebuilt in 1887.
WROCKWARDINE WOOD - Holy Trinity - 1833 by Samuel Smith. Brick, later apse.
YOCKLETON - Holy Trinity - 1861 by Edward Haycock Junior.

PRIVATE CHAPELS

EARDISTON - 1860 by Rhode Hawkins. Nave & chancel with small north tower.
GREAT OXENBOLD - 13th century, blocked lancets. House of the priors of Wenlock.

FURTHER READING

Churches of Shropshire, D.H.S.Cranage, 1901 (four vols).
Shropshire (Little Guides series), J.E.Auden, 1912.
Shropshire (Buildings of England series), N. Pevsner, 1958.
The Victoria County History of Shropshire (several vols).

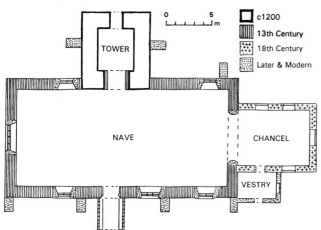

Plan of Worthen Church

Neen Sollars Church

GLOSSARY OF ARCHITECTURAL TERMS

Abacus	- A flat slab on top of a capital.
Apse	- Semi-circular or polygonal east end of a church containing an altar.
Ashlar	- Masonry of blocks with even faces and square edges.
Ballflower	- Globular flower of three petals enclosing a ball. Current c1310-40.
Baroque	- A whimsical and odd form of the Classical architectural style.
Beakhead	- Decorative motif of bird or beast heads, often biting a roll moulding.
Broaches	- Sloping half pyramids adapting an octagonal spire to a square tower.
Cable Moulding	- Norman moulding imitating a twisted cord.
Chancel	- The eastern part of a church used by the clergy.
Chevron Ornament	- A Norman ornament with continuous Vs forming a zig-zag.
Clerestory	- An upper storey pierced by windows lighting the floor below.
Collar Beam	- A tie-beam used higher up near the apex of the roof.
Crossing Tower	- A tower built on four arches in the middle of a cruciform church.
Cruciform Church	- A cross-shaped church with transepts forming the arms of the cross.
Cusp	- A projecting point between the foils of a foiled Gothic arch.
Dado	- The decorative covering of the lower part of a wall or screen.
Decorated	- The architecture style in vogue in England c1300-1380.
Dog Tooth	- Four-cornered stars placed diagonally and raised pyramidally.
Easter Sepulchre	- A recess in a chancel which received an effigy of Christ at Easter.
Elizabethan	- Of the time of Queen Elizabeth I (1558-1603).
Fan Vault	- Vault with fan-like patterns. In fashion from c1440 to 1530.
Foil	- A lobe formed by the cusping of a circle or arch.
Four Centred Arch	- A low, flattish arch with each curve drawn from two compass points.
Hammerbeam Roof	- Roof carried on arched braces set on beams projecting from a wall.
Head Stops	- Heads of humans or beasts forming the ends of a hoodmould.
Herringbone Masonry	- Courses of stones alternately sloping at 45 degrees to horizontal.
Hoodmould	- A projecting moulding above a lintel or arch to throw off water.
Impost	- A wall bracket, often moulded, to support one end of an arch.
Intrados	- The interior or lower line of a surface of an arch or vault.
Jacobean	- Of the time of King James I (1603-25).
Jamb	- The side of a doorway, window, or other opening.
King-post	- A post connecting a tie-beam or collar-beam with the roof ridge beam.
Lancet	- A long and comparatively narrow window with a pointed head.
Light	- A compartment of a window.
Lintel	- A horizontal stone or beam spanning an opening.
Miserichord	- Bracket underneath hinged choir stall seat to support standing person.
Mullion	- A vertical member dividing the lights of a window.
Nave	- The part of a church in which the congregation sits or stands.
Nook-shaft	- A column set in the angle of a pier or respond or jamb of an opening.
Norman	- A division of English Romanesque architecture from 1066 to 1200.
Ogival Arch	- Arch of oriental origin with both convex and concave curves.
Perpendicular	- The architectural style in vogue in England c1380-1540.
Pilaster	- Flat buttress or pier attached to a wall.
Piscina	- A stone basin used for rinsing out holy vessels after a mass.
Queen-posts	- Two vertical struts placed symmetrically on a tie-beam or collar-beam.
Quoins	- Dressed stones at the corners of a building.
Rere-Arch	- An arch on the inside face of a window embrasure or doorway.
Respond	- A half pier or column bonded into a wall and carrying an arch.
Reticulation	- Tracery with a net-like appearence. Current c1330-70.
Rococo	- The latest phase of the Baroque style, current in England c1720-60.
Rood Screen	- A screen with a crucifix mounted on it between a nave and chancel.
Sedilia	- Seats for clergy (usually three) in the south wall of a chancel.
Sheila-na-gig	- A female fertility symbol with the legs wide open to serve the vulva.
Spandrel	- The surface between two arches or between an arch and a corner.
Squint	- Opening allowing the main altar to be seen from a subsiderary one.
Tester	- A sounding board above a 17th or 18th century pulpit.
Tie-Beam	- A beam connecting the slopes of a roof at or near its foot.
Tracery	- Intersecting ribwork in the upper part of a later Gothic window.
Tryptych	- Three surfaces, usually sculpted or painted, joined by hinges.
Tympanum	- The space between the lintel of a doorway and the arch above it.
Vesica Window	- An oval window with a pointed head and foot.
Wall Plate	- A timber laid longitudinally along the top of a wall.
Wind Braces	- The struts used to strengthen the sloping sides of a roof.